Gay
MANNERS
and
ETIQUETTE

"A humorous, wonderfully absorbing,
and very necessary document for our times."

—Joseph Olshan,
author of *Clara's Heart*
and *Nightswimmer*

Also by Steven Petrow

DANCING AGAINST THE DARKNESS:
A Journey Through America in the Age of AIDS
ENDING THE IIIV EPIDEMIC:
Community Strategies in Disease Prevention
and Health Promotion
(EDITOR)
WHEN SOMEONE YOU KNOW HAS AIDS:
A Practical Guide
(REVISED EDITION)

The
ESSENTIAL
BOOK OF
Gay
MANNERS
and
ETIQUETTE

*A Handbook of Proper Conduct and Good
Behavior for the Gay Gentleman*

STEVEN PETROW
with Nick Steele

HarperPerennial

A Division of HarperCollinsPublishers

The text of the wedding invitation on p. 93 is reprinted by permission of Warner Books/New York from *Straight from the Heart*, copyright © 1994 by Bob Jackson-Paris and Rod Jackson-Paris.

HarperCollins books may be purchased for educational, business, or sales promotional use. For information please call or write: Special Markets Department, HarperCollins Publishers, Inc., 10 East 53rd Street, New York, NY 10022.

FIRST EDITION

Designed by C. Linda Dingler

Library of Congress Cataloging-in-Publication Data

Petrow, Steven.
    The essential book of gay manners & etiquette : a handbook of proper conduct and good behavior for the gay gentleman / by Steven Petrow with Nick Steele. — 1st ed.
        p.   cm.
    Includes index.
    ISBN 0-06-095079-X
    1. Gay men—United States—Social conditions. 2. Gay men—United States—Sexual behavior. 3. Etiquette for men—United States. 4. Dating (Social customs)—United States. 5. Gay male couples—United States—Social conditions. I. Steele, Nick, 1933–   . II. Title.
HQ 76.2.U5P43   1995
395'.142'08664—dc20   95-14647

95 96 97 98 99 ❖/RRD 10 9 8 7 6 5 4 3 2 1

For Julie and Jay, with love

—SP

To my family and dear friends Signe Mauerstein,
Anthony Compton, Jim Canfield, Tami Trost, Teddy
Kali das, and Mary Kay Kreft

And to S.B.W., I miss you

—NS

"A gentleman is one who never hurts anyone's feelings unintentionally."

—Oscar Wilde

CONTENTS

THREE
COMMITTED RELATIONSHIPS 77

INTRODUCTION

I remember being six years old watching television as Jacqueline Kennedy emerged from Saint Matthew's Cathedral in Washington, D.C. In her widow's weeds, she clutched the hands of her two small children and watched the pallbearers carry her husband's casket down the stone steps to the caisson. It was a day of national mourning, and she stood mostly composed, largely dry-eyed, and unquestionably sustained by the precision of funerary ritual. To me the overriding lesson of that day was this: At a time of total personal devastation, alone and vulnerable, Mrs. Kennedy relied upon etiquette to perform its greatest service. It gave form, ritual, and rules that could be *depended upon* to assist her through even the most troublous situation.

When faced with an etiquette dilemma, I often ask myself jokingly, "What would Jackie do?" Of course, my underlying question is actually "What is the proper form here?" Now I am not an excruciatingly correct homosexual, nor do I follow form for form's sake. I seek form and rules to help me when I'm uncomfortable or at a loss.

Still, this book is not a delineation of petty rules and regulations attempting to govern—or worse, homogenize—gay life. Nor is it an attempt to establish the ideal of what's proper gay behavior. Frankly, there's no room today for moralizing in an etiquette guide.

Let me answer the question people always ask: Just what is *gay* etiquette? Well, gay etiquette is like all etiquette and like no other etiquette. We are a largely self-invented community. Gay etiquette reflects our values and beliefs. It is based on our shared codes of behavior and ritual. It is about consideration for others, making them comfortable, being comfortable yourself, and doing the right thing. No existing manners or etiquette book does this for us.

I depend upon the rules of gay etiquette in all situations. From something as basic as what to wear to a charity benefit or a ceremony of commitment, or knowing how to introduce my boyfriend, sweetie, lover (or whatever I call my guy), to more serious situations, such as coming out, the rules of courtship, and confronting homophobia. In the age of AIDS, gay etiquette stretches beyond mere manners. It is about negotiating safer sex, disclosing HIV status, being there for our friends, saying good-bye, and arranging a funeral or memorial service.

The Essential Book of Gay Manners and Etiquette is for all gay men, however identified: gay, homosexual, or queer. It's for urban singles and suburban couples; Gen-X guys and baby boomers; sweater queens, leathermen, and activists.

I hope this book gives you the necessary tools, language, and rules to live more comfortably in the gay community and beyond—practical advice for real-life situations—something to depend on when you need it. And when in doubt, as I often am, try to apply Louis Armstrong's simple yet brilliant credo: "I got a simple rule about everybody. If you don't treat me right—shame on you!"

STEVEN PETROW

ONE

THE
ESSENTIALS

Dear Miss Manners:

What am I supposed to say when I am intro-duced to a homosexual couple?

Gentle Reader:
"How do you do?" "How do you do."

—JUDITH MARTIN, MISS MANNERS' GUIDE TO
EXCRUCIATINGLY CORRECT BEHAVIOR

*A*t the dawn of the 1980s, Judith Martin (aka Miss Manners) made etiquette history by posting the first openly homosexual entry into a manners guide. It's hard to imagine how revolutionary this act was—rescuing gay men (lesbians came later) from the dark shadows of society—but indeed it was radical. The venerable blue-hairs of the manners business—Emily Post and Amy Vanderbilt—had certainly dealt with homosexuals in a tidy manner, which is to say not at all. Still, the more contemporary mistresses of the trade—Charlotte Ford, Letitia Baldrige, and Judith Martin—collectively have but a dozen references to gays and lesbians. Not surprisingly, all of them are about our relationships with heterosexuals, or, more precisely, how straight people can "do the right thing" by us.

Frankly, that's not good enough or helpful enough. Our manners questions and etiquette problems are unique to our community and its diverse membership: What's the right word to call your lover (or is it boyfriend, companion, or spouse)? How do you confront blatant (or subtle) homophobia? How do you deal with inappropriate familiarity or sexual harassment? Is it okay to display a photograph of your lover at the office? What can you do about friends who adhere to "gay time"? These essential questions, and more, are laid out and answered here for newly "out" members of the community as well as the gay cosmopolite.

INTRODUCTIONS

The Unbreakable Rules of Introductions

Wesley strolled along Pennsylvania Avenue with Zoe, his golden retriever, peering into shop windows. Glancing into a men's clothing store, he noticed a lanky bearded man heading toward the door. "He's just my type," Wesley said to himself, as the guy headed right for him. As the handsome stranger got to the doorway, he nodded at Wesley, but suddenly the dog had other ideas—chasing at a passing bus and, sadly, dragging Wesley along with him. By the time Wesley could turn back, the bearded man had turned the corner. Two days later, Wesley spotted the same guy at a party and pointed him out to a friend. "It's fate. Go talk with him," the friend urged. Said Wesley: "I'm not sure. Besides, what would I say?"

Introductions are the foundation of all personal relations. You'll never get anywhere if people don't know your name and if you don't know theirs. How you find it out—or get found out—is up to you, but traditional introductions go a long way in making this happen.

Rule: If no one else takes the initiative, make the intro-duction happen. "Hi, I'm John Kinsey. Nice to meet you."

Rule: Introduce yourself fully and listen carefully to other people's names (it will make asking them out a whole lot easier). Whenever possible repeat names back; this is likely to make it easier to recall them in the future. To John Kinsey you'd respond: "John, it's a pleasure. I'm Tom Masters."

Rule: Hosts are obligated to introduce their guests to one another. As a host, lead your latest arrival around the room or party, saying, "I'd like you to meet Tom Masters." (Unless it's a really big party. In that case, make a couple of quick introductions, leaving Tom to meet the other Dicks and Harrys.)

Rule: Introduce "inferiors" to "superiors," which in the modern age means younger to older (your boyfriend to your mother—usually), lesser rank to higher rank (a colleague to your boss), and everyone to royalty.

Introducing Your Ex to Your New Boyfriend

If you're best friends with your ex, skip this entry. No doubt you treat him like a normal human being. It's those exes that we're not best friends with that cause problems. For instance, Jamie recalls being at a rave with his new boyfriend, Will ("smart, hunky, and sensi-tive"), when he saw his ex zeroing in on them. "I really didn't want to speak with him," said Jamie. "But that

THE ESSENTIALS

wasn't an option. There he was in my face."

Introducing your current beau to an ex is never easy to do, but it has to be done. Here's how. Take your boyfriend's hand and say to your ex: "Roger Rotten, I'd like you to meet William Wonderful. Roger, this is William." That's it. No explanations, no histories. By holding your new friend's hand and introducing him to your ex, you've made clear your current affections and priorities. Bonus points!

Rule: If you see it's inevitable, make the first move. It's always better to be proactive than reactive.

Rule: If you want to get back together with your old boyfriend, leave the new one at home.

"Those who have mastered etiquette, who are entirely, impeccably right, would seem to arrive at a point of exquisite dullness."

—DOROTHY PARKER

Surviving the Social Blackout

Ricardo and his lover, Craig, were sipping mineral water in a dark corner of a bar they frequent when a former boyfriend of Craig's approached, greeting Craig by name and—to his horror—with a wet kiss on the lips. Unable to remember the man's name, Craig couldn't

THE ESSENTIAL BOOK OF *Gay* MANNERS and ETIQUETTE

make the usual introductions, creating an awkward silence ("It seemed like thirteen days!"). "I was furious at Craig after the guy finally left," said Ricardo. "Even if he didn't remember his name, he could have done something." What could have been done?

First, some questions: Was Ricardo angry because he wasn't properly introduced, because of the wet kiss, or because this man represented Craig's past? Although it's important to take people at their word ("even if he didn't remember his name . . ."), it's smart to think about other realistic possibilities. Anyway, let's assume Craig was suffering from a total and horrifying social blackout. What could be done? He could have turned to the no-name man and said: "I don't believe you've met my lover, Ricardo." Mr. No-Name then could have answered: "Why, no, I haven't. I'm Randy No-Name." Or Craig could have confessed that he had totally forgotten Randy's name, allowing Randy to introduce himself or Ricardo to say: "I'm Ricardo, Craig's *lover*."

Rule: If you blank on a name (which everyone does from time to time), come clean. We're all human.

Rule: Everyone present has the responsibility to facilitate introductions and conversations. If your boyfriend or lover is in a jam, help him out. If you meet someone who appears to have forgotten your name, don't say: "You don't remember me, do you?" without giving your name. In fact, unless someone greets you by name, say: "I'm Hank Greene," and if that doesn't do the trick, "We met at the museum on World AIDS Day last year."

Rule: Don't ignore someone because you can't remember his name. In those cases, smile, nod, or touch the guy's arm in a friendly manner.

Avoiding the Introduction Altogether

Sad to say, very rarely are you allowed to skip the introduction. If the idea of a particular introduction makes you uncomfortable, that's a good sign that you have to do it. Whether we like it or not, ex-tricks, ex-boyfriends, and ex-lovers simply cannot be banished— nor, for that matter, can hateful family members. You may wish these people no longer existed, you may even say awful things about them in private, but when in their presence, behave properly, which is to say, make the proper introduction and mind the rest of your manners. There are, however, certain exceptions.

Rule: If you're at a huge party or a club, be selective in your introductions. (It's always a good idea to carry around your business card and hand it out freely if you're not introduced or simply can't be heard. A caution: Diehard manners mavens warn against distributing business cards at social functions. They say it's vulgar to mix business with pleasure.)

Rule: If someone is leaving an event, forget about introducing yourself and let him go. (Unless you've been dying to meet him. In that case, do an about-face

and follow him out. Ask to share a cab to wherever.
Walk with him to the subway. Do whatever it takes
to begin a conversation.)

Rule: *Don't interrupt a conversation to introduce yourself.*
(Let's say three handsome gents are arguing about
the topic du jour—endlessly. Unfortunately, you just
can't break in with: "Hello, I'm . . ." No one will, or
should, pay you any mind).

Rule: *Don't barge in on two guys who are in Stage 1 of*
heavy flirtation. They don't need a third wheel; nei-
ther will be interested in talking with you.

Rule: *You're not obliged to introduce your therapist, men*
you've met previously at a sex club or "park," or
anyone you've obtained a restraining order against.

The Intentional Cut

"It was the first Christmas after I had broken up with
Ryan," says Peter. "I knew he had been invited to the
same party, but I was determined not to speak to him, or
even look at him. I had this whole fantasy: He saunters
up to me while I'm chatting with some other people. He
keeps trying to break into the conversation, but we pretend like he's not there. He stands there like an idiot.
He's crushed."

Be warned. Fantasies are fine, but the extreme behavior described in this scenario is generally only acceptable in bad novels and Bette Davis movies. When you've
been hurt, you want to hurt back, and one of those ways

is to act out. Unfortunately, in real life (as opposed to reel life), such behavior is not acceptable. Nor is it advisable for you to storm off when an ex or other "enemy" suddenly appears; this action will only embarrass you and any others present.

Rule: Don't attend an event if you know you're going to be in the presence of someone you truly do not want to see. If that's not possible—and you find yourself face-to-face—then make do with a quick "How are you?" or a high-speed nod, and move on.

Rule: Whenever possible, take the high ground. If you snub someone in public, you'll wind up looking worse than the person you are cutting. Without knowing your joint history, others will simply view your actions as bad behavior. In short, think it, don't do it.

The Right Answer to "How Are You?"

Nine times out of ten, the casual acquaintance asking this question doesn't really want to know. It's only a conversation starter. Answer: "Fine, thanks, how are you?" In case you're tempted, the question doesn't allow you to give a full rundown of your latest therapy session, the lowdown on your incredibly dysfunctional family, or a bedside report on your soon-to-be-ex-lover. On the other hand, with close friends—who you know genuinely care about you and with whom you have a more intimate relationship—such topics are fine. Be as melodramatic as you please with your nearest and dearest.

Rule: Don't take this question seriously. Learn how to distinguish friend from faux.

Rule: Don't ask this question of someone you know to be ill if you're not willing to learn the truth about his health—emotional or physical. If you've asked, be prepared to listen.

SOCIAL STUDIES

Boyfriend? Lover? Companion?

"Most of the time," says Herb Moses (who lives with and loves Congressman Barney Frank), "I say 'friend.' But I try to say it with a capital F. Until we decide on a term and define it for the world, no phrase will feel comfortable. Gay men and lesbians need a term that would do for us what 'Ms.' did for women."

If there's any one question people want an answer to, this is it: What do I call my guy when I need to introduce him? Here's the bad news. There's no right answer to this problem—no one right word. Even Miss Manners has punted on this question, referring to it as the "Great Insolvable Etiquette Problem." What are the choices? To start: *date, boyfriend, friend, lover, companion, longtime companion, constant companion, significant other, partner, sweetie, spouse, husband. . . .*

Then, there's the problem of what these words actually mean. For instance, Tom and Ralph have been together a total of three weeks and introduce each other as "lover." It's a good bet that in another couple of weeks these guys will be "ex-lovers." Dimitri and Joey, on the other hand, have been dating for two months and Dimitri still refers to Joey as his "boyfriend candidate." Still, there's another couple—together more than a decade—who refer to one another as "my friend."

Rule: *Talk to your guy about what he wants to be called and tell him how you'd like to be referred to. Talk about whether that choice is different at a dinner with gay friends, out at a bar together, or at a mixed workplace function. Some couples choose to use "boyfriend" or "lover" in a gay context and "partner," "companion," or "friend" in a more mainstream crowd. Others find these types of distinctions abhorrent, arguing that the ambiguity of the terms purposely and negatively camouflages the true nature of the relationship. In the end, it's more important that both of you are comfortable with your terms of affection than anyone else.*

Rule: *Don't be cloying, using language that tells others more than they need to know about your private (and sex) life.*

Rule: *Don't make up a word. POSSLQ (persons of the opposite sex sharing living quarters) never worked for heterosexuals; we can't imagine what our talented brothers might contrive.*

Rule: Although this question can take up endless hours of a couple's time (not to mention too many dinner parties), don't let it. There are many more important things—such as how you feel about him—than what you call him.

Inappropriate Familiarity

For the record, we *love* appropriate familiarity. But we hate inappropriate familiarity: a too-soon buss, a crafty hand on the knee, a confession of "true" love (*especially* after but two dates), any information from a waiter beyond the specials (and maybe his first name), and terms of endearment from people we don't hold dear.

Rule: Refer to people by the name they use themselves. Listen.

Rule: Don't use darling, sweetheart, baby, girlfriend, babycakes, honey unless you have an intimate relationship with that person or unless you're truly terrible with names.

Rule: Respect people's space. Don't touch, kiss, fondle, or stroke if you think such gestures won't be appreciated.

The Art of the Apology

Summertime and the living is easy. Well, mostly. But for Tomás this particular garden party proved ruinous. Wearing his spanking new white linen suit, Tomás knew he looked fabulous. It had certainly cost him enough. Picking at the appetizers and sipping red wine while telling a joke, Tomás didn't see his soon-to-be-ex-friend Larry behind him. Like a slo-mo car accident, the two men backed into each other—the wine flying all over Tomás's suit, staining it, and turning his face an even bloodier color. Larry, almost freakishly, went unscathed. After quickly surveying the damage to Tomás, Larry said bluntly, "It's not my fault."

You've heard all the excuses before. He stands you up ("It wasn't my fault"). He insults your friends ("It wasn't my fault"). He forgets your birthday ("It wasn't my fault"). Yes, sometimes it's not your fault. But even when it's not, there's no harm (and much to gain) in apologizing.

Rule: If you've wronged someone, acknowledge it and then make up for it. The best way is to start with your basic, flat-out apology (which does not imply guilt, liability, or the need to redress further): "I'm sorry."

Rule: Be specific in your apology. "I'm sorry I have to cancel our date so late. This work project is just so out of hand. Can I make this up to you next week?" Even better: "May I take you out next week?" If this is someone you're sweet on, send a bunch of his favorite flowers.

Rule: As the severity of the infraction increases, so too does the price. The curve goes something like this:

spoken apology, written apology, candy, flowers, little gifts, big gifts. Don't be stingy with your apologies. (See also "Notes of Apology," p. 147.)

"Punctuality is the politeness of kings."

—Louis XVIII

Gay Time

"Another ginger ale?" the waiter asked Max.

"That would be fine," he answered, checking his watch for the fourth time.

Max was certain that Hank had said eight o'clock. It was already eight-fifteen and no Hank. He checked his messages—still no word. He wondered if something had happened, or was he waiting at the wrong café? How long should he wait? Finally, Hank strolled in at eight-thirty-five with a sheepish smile and offered: "Sorry, the time just got away from me. What looks good?"

Gay men are so frequently late that everyone's been burned by "gay time." It's so prevalent it's become an accepted part of gay culture. Even worse is the cavalier attitude that often accompanies such tardiness. Time is a valuable commodity, and it's inconsiderate to friends and colleagues to make them wait.

Rule: Arrive within ten minutes of the designated time if meeting at a public place. Call ahead if you know

*you will be late. If more than a couple of minutes
late, apologize. Explain why you're late. Mirror
time, like gay time, doesn't cut it.*

Rule: *If waiting, allow twenty minutes. Then you're foot-
loose and fancy free.*

Rule: *If an emergency arises and you won't be able to make
it at all, call ahead, leave a message on his answering
machine, page him—try to reach him as best you
can.*

"Everyone thinks himself wellbred."

—LORD SHAFTSBURY

Rules for Dealing With Unpleasant Types

From the bore to the bigot, the egotist, the know-it-
all, and the drunk, gay life has got its cast of difficult
characters. The question is: How do you deal with these
people civilly and, more important, how do you dispatch
them completely? All these types have one thing in common: They have no idea how offensive other people per-
ceive them to be. Consequently, they require an extraordinary amount of tact and finesse.

THE BORE: The least offensive in this category, but still
not your person of choice to be seated next to at a din-

ner or cornered by at a party. The bore can talk and talk
and talk and really never say anything.

*Rule: If seated next to a bore, talk to your other dinner
companions or find a discussion for the entire group
to participate in. Hosts should never put two bores
next to each other or, for that matter, two incredibly
shy people.*

*Rule: Never stand in a corner (or sit where you can't
quickly escape) if you have any reason to think a
bore may be roaming the premises.*

*Rule: Invoke the five-minute rule. After someone's bent
your ear more than that, feel free to check out.*

THE BIGOT: This is one type we won't knowingly social-
ize with. The idea that a gay man, who ought to know
something about oppression and prejudice, would dis-
criminate against others is shameful and appalling.

*Rule: Let a bigot know that what he is saying is offensive
to you (whether it's about women, people of color,
heterosexuals, bisexuals, Jews . . .). Until a bigot is
called a bigot, he will think it's okay to mouth off.*

*Rule: Once you've said your piece, take your leave.
There's no reason to continue to engage in social
niceties. Hate and prejudice are dangerous, but tol-
erance of them is even more insidious.*

> ## "Do you wish men to speak well of you?
> ## Then never speak well of yourself."
>
> —Blaise Pascal

THE EGOTIST: "But enough about me . . ." Let's set the record straight: This kind of guy has got to go. There's nothing more unattractive than a fellow who can talk only about himself, look at himself in the mirror, and sing his own praises.

Rule: Don't try to change the subject; the egotist will always find a way to bring the focus back to himself. Either tell a very long story, which will deprive the egotist of his platform, or just get away as quickly as you possibly and politely can.

THE KNOW-IT-ALL: He corrects your grammar. He can list all the kings and queens of England in reverse order. He has perfect manners and lets you know that. After you've listened to him, you wonder how you made it through third grade.

Rule: Never compete with a know-it-all. They always win, always have, and always will. And if they don't, they find ways of making it seem as if they have.

*Rule: Be secure. Everyone knows they're overcompensat-
ing. When corrected, flash your best smile, add a
gracious thanks, and say good-bye.*

THE DRUNK: There's nothing funny about a friend or
colleague who is drunk in public. While he may be rude
or offensive, your job is to separate him from the crowd
and let him recover in private (and safely).

*Rule: Try not to take to heart what a drunk says. He's
drunk, remember. Conversely, just because he won't
remember what he said doesn't mean you have to
forget. You can always address what the wine forced
out of him at a later, more sober time.*

*Rule: Never let someone who's had too much to drink
drive home. Take his keys. Call his boyfriend. Hail a
cab. Provide a warm place for him to sleep it off.*

Public Displays of Affection

Jock and Luis had gone on a daylong hike two hours
north of San Francisco. Walking through the spring
flowers, the two fellows intermittently held hands along
the trail. "We were shocked by the looks people gave
us," said Jock. "You'd think holding hands was a revolutionary act. You'd think we were having sex in front of
them. Was there something inappropriate about this?"

A few years before we had also heard another relevant
story on public displays of affection. "George and I had

been visiting my family for the holidays, along with my brother and sister and their spouses," said Jasper. "Like my siblings, George and I held hands from time to time and even kissed each other on the cheek. Late in the day, my mother took me aside and said sternly: 'There'll be no touching in this house.' I said, 'Does that apply only to George and me or to everyone—including the heterosexuals?' That stymied her."

First, we're entirely in favor of these kinds of PDA. But let's talk about open-mouth kissing in restaurants and sex on the beach (we didn't say in the dunes). In short, too much. Over the line. Even in an entirely gay crowd, show a little decorum. Believe us, no one wants to see this kind of behavior—unless, of course, they've paid to see it.

Rule: Showing affection publicly is the same for gays as it is for straights. No matter where, hand-holding, eye gazing, and light kissing are acceptable behaviors. However, when in public, be wary of open-mouth kissing, excessive fondling, and having sex.

"*As the purse is emptied, the heart is filled.*"

—VICTOR HUGO

Charity Events

In the midst of the fall benefit season, Bill found himself holding a handful of invitations, wondering whether he'd ever be invited to a party that wasn't a benefit. "I've got all these friends who think nothing of inviting me to spend $75 for a dinner event but don't ever just invite me to their place. What's my obligation to attend these events?" he asks.

Obviously the gay community needs all the support it can get, with many nonprofits relying on dinners, parties, and other events for their operating income. Still, the number of events and the cost continue to skyrocket. In a perfect world, you'd sit down once a year, figure out exactly how much you could afford to give, and write the checks. But there are limits. If every time you open the mailbox you see an invitation that will cost you big bucks, you're bound to run out of patience and funds. This kind of situation winds up being counterproductive for everyone.

Rule: Be judicious in the number of benefits you attend, and equally careful in the number of benefit invitations you send.

Rule: Choose specific organizations and charities that you support. Make a commitment to them and leave the rest to others.

Rule: There are ways to give other than writing a check. Donating your time, services, or goods can make a much-needed contribution.

Rule: Don't be embarrassed to pass on an invitation, whether it's because you can't afford it or because you choose not to support the charity.

Asking Someone to Join You

Cozying up to someone at a bar is one thing. Making an approach on the street is also pretty straightforward. But how do you extend an invitation from tableside? Andy was having dinner alone at a trendy gay spot in Miami when he spied an attractive man standing by the bar. After several moments of intense eye contact, Andy was embarrassed and picked up his copy of *Vanity Fair* and began reading at warp speed, keeping one eye on the guy. Again, their eyes locked. What should he do now? Andy wondered.

The easiest and most risk-free way to approach the situation is to jot a note on a business card (something simple but direct, like "Would you care to join me?") and ask the waiter to deliver it. You could also send over a drink. All that eye contact either means the guy is interested . . . or hungry; in either case, Andy should be successful in snagging a dinner partner. If that seems too forward, or the guy doesn't take the initiative himself, it's perfectly fine for Andy to head off to the john, making sure that his route goes directly by the bar, where he could introduce himself, chat a bit, and then ask if his new friend would like to join him. *Bon appétit!* (Caveat emptor: If he does join you, be prepared to treat him to dinner.)

Who Pays on a Date?

You've finally gotten up the nerve to ask that someone special to dinner. Now it's time to pay the price. It used to be that the man paid for the woman. Well, even straights can't live by that rule anymore. If you invite him out to dinner, you have two responsibilities: proposing a restaurant and footing the bill.

Years ago, Jim was invited by a very dapper writer to a film opening. Of course, he said yes—both because he wanted to go out with this guy and because he'd never been to a Hollywood premiere before. About a week after he said yes, the phone rang; it was his date, Jules Cinema-Verité. "I've bought the tickets. They came to $125 each. You can give me a check when we go out." Jim was speechless. He wishes he had said: "What? $125? You cheap sonofabitch. Of course, you're paying for me." Or, something a tad more composed: "I'm sorry that I didn't understand that you expected me to pay for this date. Because you invited me, I assumed you were taking me. Unfortunately, I won't be able to make it."

Rule: Both guys should understand who is going to pay before the date takes place. Picking an expensive eaterie (or event) and then expecting to go dutch isn't a good way to get a second date.

Rule: If you find you need to borrow money from your date, pay him back within twenty-four hours if at all possible.

Rule: If, in fact, you pay the first time, then it's up to him to offer to pick up the next one. But first he has to ask you out.

Rule: If your date pays for you, you are not obliged either to have sex with him or to ask him out.

"[Sociability is] the art of unlearning to be preoccupied with yourself."

—OSKAR BLUMENTHAL

Dividing the Bill

Let's make sure we understand the problem. You've had a $12 entrée and he's had a $10 one. Do you pay $2 more? No, let it go. Presumably, the next time or the time after, he'll order a salad or a dessert and you'll be ahead a couple of dollars.

But what happens to the guy who's watching both his pocketbook and his waistline? Sal and his good friend Roberto used to go out for dinner about twice a month. "Roberto was both a big spender and big eater," Sal recalls. "We'd go out and I'd order chicken-this or chicken-that, ice water, and coffee. That's all I wanted and, frankly, that's all I could afford. The problem was that Roberto would order every course—from the shrimp cocktail to the crème brûlée, with steak frites and a salad in between—and a couple of cocktails. Then, when the bill came, he'd grab it, add on a generous tip, and divide by two. I felt like I was subsidizing him."

Yes, Sal was providing major funding for Roberto's diet. In the best of all worlds, Roberto would grab the check, add up his own hefty part, and put that amount down, saying, "I had a little more than you. My part is $49.75. Yours comes to about $13.50." Unfortunately, this rarely happens. Sal, however, is encouraged to pick up the tab and do likewise: "My share is about $13.50," he says, putting his money down on the table and passing the bill back to his friend. Roberto is then obliged to carry his own weight.

Rule: If the bill is under $50 and the discrepancy $5 or less, share the tab.

Rule: When the discrepancy is significant, don't be shy about pointing that out. Friends and lovers should not take advantage of others' generosity or reluctance to talk about money.

Rule: If you have benefited from the division of the tab, take your friend out the next time (or at least buy him a drink).

"A host is like a general: It takes a mishap to reveal his genius."

—HORACE

Restaurant Birthday Bashes

"Eighteen of us were invited to Sperry's thirtieth birthday at a charming, but not too pricey, French restaurant," Reed recalls. "I figured it would be the usual drill. Everyone sings happy birthday off key, buys a fun present, and chips in for the birthday boy's dinner. Not quite. When the check came, the 'host' made like Casper and it was left to me to figure the tip and do the division. Problem No. 1: One couple had already left, throwing down an insufficient number of bills on the table. Problem No. 2: Another guest announced to me, 'You know it's my birthday this week.' And having said that, never opened his wallet. Problem No. 3: Two recovering alcoholics came over and quietly told me they weren't going to pay for anyone's liquor bill ('it makes us uncomfortable'). I found myself asking people to contribute $50 each, double what it should have been if the entire bill had been equally divided. By the time we finished paying, the bash was ruined."

No doubt about it, restaurant bashes seem designed to send you directly to bankruptcy court. No matter how much or how little money you go in with, you'll come out empty-handed. If people aren't ducking their tabs, they're ordering the most expensive items on the menu, double scotches, rare wines, and expecting the group to pay for it all. This has got to stop.

Host Rule: If a host can organize a group of people, he can also take control by determining a fixed dinner—with a fixed price—for the guests (an appetizer, choice of entrées, birthday cake, and coffee/tea). Aside from the bar bill, people can be told what dinner will total, making clear that the cost of the birthday guest's dinner will be shared.

Host Rule: Take control of the check, do the math, and discreetly inform others of their share.

Guest Rule: In accepting such an invitation, expect to pay at least what you've been told. None of this: "I only had a salad." If you have a specific objection, bring it to the host's attention in advance. No surprises at the table.

Guest Rule: To the fellow who spontaneously deems this his birthday as well: "That's fine, Jack, but this is Fred's birthday, and none of us likes you well enough to pay for your dinner." Then smile.

Guest Rule: If you don't want to conform to the host's rules, don't go.

THE WORKPLACE

"Out" on the Job

To be or not to be, that is the question. Although one of the basic premises of good etiquette is to make people feel comfortable, don't let this be marshaled as an argument for keeping you in the closet (it's based on the erroneous presumption that working around gay people will cause discomfort). No, this is a question and choice for each of us. But what does it mean to be out? Does it necessitate hanging a gay-pride flag on your desk? Does it mean referring to a boyfriend or partner (if you have one) in casual conversation? Does it mean making charitable contributions to AIDS and/or gay organizations that are then matched by your employer? Or does it mean attending an office function with another man? Obviously, there are many degrees to being out. For some, the disadvantages outweigh the advantages. Certainly your personal comfort is of primary importance; so, by the way, is your job security and advancement.

Rule: Don't legislate the schedule or the degree of someone's coming out. By the same token, don't allow yourself to be legislated. Coming out is an extremely personal decision. If possible, discuss the ramifications with trusted friends and colleagues.

Rule: Outing a colleague—intentionally or unintentionally—is a violation of that person's privacy. Don't do it!

"One face to the world, another at home, makes for misery."

—AMY VANDERBILT

Displaying Photographs

Take a good look around your office. Chances are you'll see lots of pictures of husbands, wives, girlfriends, and, of course, babies. Are they pushing their lifestyle on

you? No, these heterosexuals simply want to be surrounded by faces of their loved ones. Fine. So, presumably, do you.

Rule: *If you enjoy daydreaming about your boyfriend or
sweetie at work, put up his picture. This is not a
revolutionary act, despite what some heterosexuals
may say. What's good for the goose is good for the
gander. Explain who he is to those who ask. Let others make their own assumptions.*

Dealing With Home Crises at Work

Mack remembers how he reacted during a period
when his lover, Raul, was very sick. Over the weeks that
Raul stayed home, it became increasingly difficult for
Mack to keep his private life from infiltrating his work.
"Often I had to leave the office to run Raul over to the
doctor or the lab, or go home at lunchtime to make sure
he was eating. Of course, Raul was calling me at the
office two or three times a day as well. I had to admit it
was getting out of hand, but I couldn't see any other way
about it."

Home crises are best dealt with at home. That's not
always possible. Breakups, illness, and death are especially likely to spill over into the office. No one is asking
for any *special* consideration, but if heterosexuals in
your office are given time off to assist a family member
or spouse, you have every moral right to demand equal
treatment (you may not have a legal right). That's a fundamental element of the gay rights movement. This may

take some explaining to your boss or coworkers. "Raul is my family," you could say in describing why you are leaving work to take him to the hospital. "If I don't take him, he won't get treatment."

Rule: *Make your case. If others don't see it, point out how everyone must, at one time or another, bring his home problems into the office or take time off to deal with them. Consistency is the basis of equality.*

Rule: *If someone in your office needs assistance or a show of support, take the lead in organizing it. This means more than sending a card. A good precedent goes a long way.*

"*Manners are more important than the laws. Upon them, in a great measure, the laws depend.*"

—EDMUND BURKE

Confronting Homophobia

After a three-day weekend, Isaac returned to his law office to find the photograph of his lover defaced with the word "faggot" written across it. Outraged, he went to the managing partner and explained what had happened. The senior attorney asked what he should do. Isaac responded: "At the next staff meeting, I'd like you to tell people what happened, making clear that this is not acceptable behavior at this firm." The managing partner did just that. Three weeks later the photograph was again defaced. This time the senior attorney told Isaac: "We're going to install a hidden mini-cam in your office. We're determined to stop this now." The perpetrator was eventually caught.

At a staff meeting of a national magazine, one of the editors told this joke to the assembled staffers: "What is the longest bridge in the world?" she asked brightly. No one answered. "The Oakland–San Francisco Bay Bridge," she volunteered, adding, "It goes from Africa to Fairyland." Not bad: racist and homophobic all in one. One of the staffers, a young gay reporter, wondered how to deal with the problem—in fact, whether he had the right if not the duty to protest.

Sometimes homophobia is as blatant and terrifying as physical violence; other times it can be less overt, but no less injurious: a passed-over promotion or reaching the metaphoric "glass ceiling." Clearly, homophobia has many guises.

Rule: Homophobia (or racism) is never acceptable and should always be met head-on, either by confronting the perpetrator (publicly or in private) or speaking to a superior about the problem.

Rule: Deal with verbal defamation immediately. If someone makes a gay joke in your presence, point out that you are not amused, that the joke is based on stereotypes, and that it is offensive to all people (not just gays).

*Rule: Report hate crimes immediately. While safety always
come first, make sure you notify the police and any
local or national groups working to prevent violence
against gays and lesbians (such as the Anti-Violence
Project in New York City, 212-807-0197).*

The Right Answer to "Are You Gay?"

A colleague approaches you at the water fountain. He fumbles for his cup and then, under his breath, whispers: "I saw you at the End-Up last night. I didn't know . . ." You panic because, while you were dancing with some beautiful men at the End-Up, you're not out at work. What do you do? What do you say?

This is a difficult decision, because it's one thing to omit certain details from your life (for instance, *"We went to the opera last night"* becomes *"I went to The Flying Dutchman"*; or "My lover is in the hospital with PCP" is transposed to "A really good friend was hospitalized") and a different matter altogether to find yourself telling out-and-out untruths. If you're thrust into a situation where lying seems like a reasonable course, step back and analyze what's happening. There's something inherently unhealthy in lying about one's true nature. If push comes to shove, tell your questioner: "This is not a work conversation." After all, you are at work.

*Rule: Don't let others attempt to violate your privacy.
Don't violate others'. If the question was asked by
your boss, it could be considered illegal.*

> ## *"The first quality of a good education is good manners—and some people flunk the course."*
>
> —HUBERT H. HUMPHREY

The Right Answer to "Is (Blank) Gay?"

Thierry, it turns out, had two secrets to reveal. In a phone chat with his gay colleague Doug, he mentioned that he was infatuated with another coworker, Bruce, and Bruce with him. Bad enough this being a work situation. But Thierry was in a monogamous relationship, and Bruce was married (to a woman). Of course, Doug was all ears, and a couple of weeks later when another gay colleague asked if Bruce was gay, Doug quickly downloaded his information. "I didn't really think about it," says Doug, who had unhesitantly divulged Bruce's secret. Not long after, Bruce learned of the indiscretion and approached Doug absolutely livid. Doug asks: "What did I do wrong?"

This is what is known as the domino effect: one transgression leading to another, leading to a virtual *scandale*. Thierry, who escaped unscathed, deserves as much if not more of Bruce's fury. After all, Thierry outed Bruce in the first place. And then Doug outed Bruce. When approached, Doug could have replied: "I really don't know. If you're that interested, ask Bruce yourself." Having made the error, Doug most certainly should apologize to Bruce. His *culpa maxima*.

Rule: Do not trade in gossip—or what some cleverly call the passing of information. Privacy about one's sexual orientation is paramount.

HOLIDAYS

Halloween

Listen to Randy's problem: "My boyfriend and I were invited to one of *those* 'makeup' parties. You start with a cocktail, shave your legs and chest, have another cocktail, then it's time to become a total glamour puss: lipstick, powder, eye shadow too. Everyone's squeezing and squealing as he slips into his evening wear. The problem is I don't get the drag thing, but my boyfriend does. He says I'm judgmental. I say I'm not comfortable."

What was that book by Marlo Thomas? *Free to Be You and Me.* Let it go, girls (and boys). Every man should do what he's comfortable doing (as long as he's not hurting someone) and leave the rest.

Rule: Halloween should be fun. Period. Dress in a way that pleases you. If you do drag, get a friend who's done it to help you look "pretty, witty, and gay."

Rule: If drag makes you uncomfortable, ask the host if it's okay to come in another costume.

Rule: If you decide to do drag on city streets, watch out for violence against gay men. Halloween brings out heterosexuals in droves to watch, gawk, and sadly, sometimes, to bash. Always go out with friends. Fashion tip: Wear a whistle around your neck and tell everyone it's your aunt's favorite pendant.

Surviving Christmas

David recalls his take on the season: "Flying to the Coast before the holidays last year, I couldn't help but think about Christmases past. I remember the year my mother descended the stairs in a palpable, white-hot fury because my sisters had already opened their gifts. A few Christmases later, I remember my uncle getting drunk and destroying the family china. Skipping forward a half-dozen years, there was the very memorable holiday dinner when one of my sisters came out and wasn't invited to the family get-together. Through all this, my job was to hold the family together, to keep the center from unraveling entirely."

Forget those Currier and Ives images of holidays past. If anything, the great holiday dash—from Thanksgiving to New Year's—raises the emotional jackpot to record highs. Family woes, loneliness, depression, money troubles, broken relationships, and painful memories of lost loved ones, all make surviving the holidays a major challenge. This stress often manifests itself in all kinds of misbehaviors.

Rule: If you're not wanted by your family or are uncomfortable with them, create your own extended family and traditions. There's no rule that says you must go home. Stay with a friend, sibling, or other relative if a full-time visit home is just too much.

Rule: If you're tangled up in the holiday blues, volunteer at a local hospital, soup kitchen, or AIDS service organization. Even if you're feeling fine, volunteer.

Rule: Reduce or eliminate the symbolism of gift giving. Money and gifts are not barometers of feelings. Buy gifts you can afford, but don't repress or curtail your expression of emotion.

Rule: Negotiate holiday schedules in advance. If you want to spend time with your lover and your family (and you can't be with both together, for whatever reason), discuss your plans in advance so that expectations are realistic.

Rule: Don't use drink, drugs, or sex to camouflage pain or loss. Talking about your own losses may not only help you feel better but could be a tremendous relief to others dealing with similar problems. If you can't work through these issues yourself or with friends, get professional help.

TWO

FRIENDS, COURTSHIP— AND SEX

The great secret is not having good manners or bad manners or any particular sort of manners, but having the same manners for all human souls.

—GEORGE BERNARD SHAW

*T*he phone rings. It's your friend—any gay friend, every gay friend at some time. He's in a panic about a "man question." You've heard the litany of situations:

"I see him every day at the gym, but how do I ask him out?"

"The guy from the supermarket called and asked *me* out on the answering machine. No, I don't want to go out with him. What do I say?"

"You wouldn't believe it. He said, 'I'm HIV-negative so we don't need to worry about condoms.' But he was *so* handsome. . . ."

"He turned out to be the most boring man I've ever had dinner with. Before coffee, I just told him I had a splitting headache and had to leave. Was that awful?"

"It was a wonderful night. How do I make sure I get another date with him?"

"I had to break a date at the last minute. I was such a boor. What should I do now?"

"I'm falling in love. How do I tell him?"

"He said, 'Do you love me?' I don't, but I didn't know what to say."

"What do I do the first time I go to a sex club? What do I wear?"

"How do I find a hustler? What's the safest way? When do I pay him?"

When it comes to meeting men, whether as potential friends, as dates, or for sex only, gay etiquette promises and delivers real-life, commonsense solutions. This chapter can't promise that you'll never spend Saturday night alone, but you'll never miss another opportunity, never fail to deliver just the right line, or know how to handle yourself in the most naked of circumstances.

FRIENDSHIP

Making Friends

Adam moved to St. Louis from Los Angeles, thinking that in a smaller city it would be easier to find friends. "I was surprised that it was as difficult in St. Louis to meet people—gay or straight—and even harder to advance from acquaintance to friendship," he explains. "Is there a trick to meeting people?"

Yes, there is a real art to making friends. You need to be out there and visible, with a positive attitude. Simplistic as it may seem, people are drawn to others who appear open, content, and happy. Meeting prospective new friends is obviously the first step. To do that, you need to take advantage of all your opportunities. Once you've met a potential friend, sharing a meal ("breaking bread") has a particular way of forging a relationship. Being invited to someone's house is a terrific compliment and a genuine sign of caring and wanting to know you better.

Rule: *If you're invited to a party, go! You never can know who will be there. At the very least, you may simply have a good time; you may make a friend or even find a date.*

Rule: *Show genuine interest in the people you meet. Listen to what people say; don't just watch their lips move while waiting for your next opening. A good listener makes a good friend. Don't make hasty judgments. It may take someone more than twenty-two seconds to warm and open up to you.*

Rule: *Step out of your everyday schedule and do something new, go someplace different. Join a health club, a political or professional association, a book club, a temple or church group—any group that interests you and that attracts other single men. Go online, use the personals. Take an extension class at your local university or sign up to volunteer at a gay or AIDS-related organization. You're bound to meet interesting, active, involved people in all these places.*

Rule: Keep an open mind. People who are different from
you could make the best of friends, but you'll never
know until you give them a chance.

"If you have one true friend, you have more than your share."

—THOMAS FULLER

Maintaining Friendships

When all is said and done, it's true that friendships matter most. But how quickly some guys toss off friends or fail to see the value in investing time and energy in them. Well, good morning. Friendships are a gift and, as such, something of great value. Expect to give a lot of time and attention to developing and maintaining friendships. Trust, the basis of all healthy relationships, builds over time and is earned through respect, loyalty, sensitivity, and caring.

Rule: Learn the art of reciprocation. If a friend does
something nice for you, find a way to pay back his
or her kindness.

Rule: Consider your friend's interests when you propose
plans.

Rule: Don't stand by and let people speak poorly of a
friend of yours. Being a loyal friend can mean com-

*ing to the defense of your friend if he (or she) is
being criticized or hassled. You have every right to
say, "Tom and I are good friends. I'd appreciate that
you not say that about him in my presence."*

Rule: *Be a friend all the time, not just when it suits you.
Stay in touch even when it's not convenient for you.*

Rule: *A true friend understands that friendships have
their highs and lows and knows the art of patience.
If your friend is starting a new romance, has a new
job, or is taking care of a sick friend, don't expect to
hear from him as often as previously.*

Rule: *A confidence shared should be a confidence kept.
Respect his privacy as you would your own. Never
gossip about your friends.*

....

"Reprove your friends in secret, praise them openly."

—PUBLILIUS SYRUS

....

Jealousy and Competition among Friends

"Tony and I have been friends for just a few months,
and although I think he's great, he does some things
that drive me crazy. What do I mean? When we go out
together, he flirts with everyone I'm interested in and
often relates purposely embarrassing stories about me.

When we meet a single guy together, he starts edging me out of the conversation as soon as he can. Later, I'm sure to hear how interested that guy was in *him not me.*"

If you find yourself competing with or jealous of your friends, something's amiss. Ask yourself, What's going on? Talk about your feelings. It's important not to let other men come between friends.

Rule: Don't flirt with a friend's boyfriend; it's like playing with matches. You don't know who's going to get burned, but it's just as likely to be you as anyone.

Rule: Before dating a friend's ex, ask the friend what he thinks. While no rational discourse will ever stop or slow the flow of hormones, make sure you have all the relevant information before you take the plunge.

Rule: Save your perfectly honed witticisms and bitchy criticisms for each other—in private.

Rule: Don't make friendship into a contest. The beauty of all friendships is that each friend imagines the other deserves the crown.

The Right Answer to "Can We Just Be Friends?"

Clark and Woodie have been dating for about three weeks. Woodie is everything Clark has hoped for in a guy—smart, successful, witty, and caring. There was potential written all over him. When Woodie invited Clark over to his place for dinner so they "could be alone to talk," Clark thought the relationship was about to get really serious. But from the moment he walked in the door with a bouquet of peonies and a fine white burgundy, Woodie seemed terribly ill at ease. He began to stammer: "The reason I wanted to talk to you is hard for me." Clark just sat there waiting to be eighty-sixed. "Clark, I like you a lot, but I don't think it's working out." After a pause, Woodie followed up: "Can we just be friends?"

This is one of the most difficult sentences to hear from someone you care about. A clichéd rejection. The problem is no matter how someone dumps you (let's call a spade a spade), you're still being dumped. When you are faced with this question, the first thing to decide is whether you want to remain friends with him. If not, exit stage left pronto. If, however, you think he's genuine in his offer and you want to make the effort to transform the relationship, tell him that, take some time off to let things settle, and then start over.

Rule: If he's given you the line, don't plead your case or ask for another chance. You may ask "why" but if he's come this far, you can be certain he's got his reasons.

Rule: Don't let anger get the better of you. Don't say "You were always lousy in bed, your friends are trash, and your dog is stupid." Don't go the revenge route either: "I'll ruin you" or some other tart reply.

Appropriate Ways to Meet Men to Date

The search. The hunt. The dating game. Consider Joe's complaint: "All I want is to go out with a man I like, have a nice dinner, go to a show, and kiss a little bit. Why does that seem so impossible?" Yes, meeting men for dates can be one of the most daunting tasks single gay men are confronted with (in contrast to meeting men for sex, which, for many, seems so easy). Although it's not all that different from meeting men for friends, it's the rare man who acts the same in a platonic situation as when on the prowl.

To meet men, consider two things: your meetability factor and the ability to be in the right place at the right time. Presentation is key to meeting people—and we're not talking about fashion or grooming here (that comes later), but how you show yourself to the world. Do you walk down the street staring at your tennis shoes, or do you take in the world as it passes? When you go to a party, do you make it a point to engage guys in conversation, hoping to strike a responsive chord, or do you stay with your own friends and gossip about everyone else? Are you an optimist or a whiner?

Rule: Flirt, flirt, flirt! Smile, wink, toss your head back, say hello while passing by, look back. . . . There are countless ways to let him know you're available.

> ## *"Confidence does more to make conversation than wit."*
>
> —La Rochefoucauld

The Pickup

How do you actually connect with a guy once your "gaydar" has honed in on him? Those first few words can be the most daunting, and if you hesitate he may be lost forever.

Take the case of Zack Clifton. Zack is at his neighborhood market, debating whether to buy the blueberry or peach low-fat yogurt, when an attractive guy steps into his aisle. Zack takes both yogurts and wonders how to meet this man. The stranger moves toward Zack, picking up a gallon of skim milk along the way. He smiles. Zack smiles back. Zack keeps walking. At the end of the aisle, he looks back and sees the stranger flash another smile in his direction. What should he do?

The smile combined with the backward glance is prima facie evidence that the stranger is interested. How does Zack finesse the introduction? He could smash his cart into the other man's (we actually know a fellow who rear-ended a convertible just to meet the driver), but it's probably easier to get on the deli or bakery line while waiting for your fat-free sliced turkey. Then talk about *anything.* "Oh, skim milk? I try to eat a low-fat diet, too." If he's looking for an excuse to talk, he'll appreciate the opening. He might even invite you over for a low-fat (but delicious) dinner.

Rule: Once face-to-face with a guy, start a conversation. Try not to worry about looking foolish. Even if he walks off in midsentence, you'll survive, and it will be good practice for the next time.

Rule: Follow through. If you've been chatting for a while, don't just let him wander off into the neighborhood. Say: "Can I give you my name and number. It'd be nice to meet for coffee or drinks sometime soon." Do it.

Blind Dates

Before Frederic could say hello, Lori was talking at warp speed: "I met this great guy at a party last night. He's handsome. He's smart. He dresses great. He's almost done with therapy! I think he'd be perfect for you," she said. Said Frederic: "Lori, I've had it with blind dates. You remember I ran the personal ad two months ago and had coffee with fourteen airheads. I've also met people off the electronic bulletin board. I think I'm meant to be single." "You haven't met anyone that I've picked out for you," she continued, pressing the stranger's case. "Okay, okay, give me his number and give him mine. We'll see."

Everyone hates blind dates. Everyone goes on blind

dates. It's as simple as that. Although this form of dating remains among the most maligned and ridiculed of dating practices, don't be closed-minded. However, your odds of having a good time are significantly higher when a friend plays matchmaker. (At least you can ask a lot of subjective questions beforehand: "*How* good-looking is he?" "What's his sense of humor like?" "Is he a fashion victim?" "Does he have good teeth?")

What happens when it doesn't work out? For some reason, many of us think that, because it was a "blind date," not only does the guy never get a second thought, but the whole form of dating is eternally damned. Remember: Don't throw out the baby with the bathwater.

Rule: Talk on the phone with all prospective blind dates. Get as much information as possible from him or your matchmaker. If looks are important (and to whom are they really not?) ask for a returnable photo if it's a personal ad, or ask your friend to show you one. If you're describing yourself, tell your best version of the truth.

Rule: Coffee dates are a very good way to start off. After half an hour, you can say either, "It was nice meeting you. I have another appointment," or "It was great meeting you. Would you like to have dinner later in the week?"

Rule: Choose a café or restaurant that is known to both of you. A familiar setting will help put both of you at ease.

Rule: Even if he doesn't hotwire you, he may be good
friend material. Besides, he might know someone
else who's just perfect for you.

Rule: Don't criticize or chastise your friend for choosing a
guy who didn't turn out to be "Mr. Right." At least
your friend tried. Do the same for your friends.

Asking Him Out

You could grow old and gray waiting for some man to ask you out. So don't. Ask him out yourself. What have you got to lose? (Oh, maybe your self-respect, your reputation, any semblance of an ego, but really what have you got to lose?) Even though you may be nervous (who isn't?), try not to appear overly anxious or too eager. Men are generally attracted to a guy who shows restraint and who can communicate without blathering. When you ask him out, be specific without pinning it down completely. "George, would you like to have dinner with me this week?" If he says yes, all you need to do is agree on which night. If he says he's busy, give him your phone number and ask him to call you (that way you can tell if he's really interested).

Make the date sound interesting—a little out of the ordinary. If your prospective date tells you that he loves foreign delicacies, say, "I know this great little Indian restaurant. The menu is completely authentic. You sit on pillows on the floor. It's very cozy. Why don't we have dinner there next weekend?"

Rule: Take chances. If someone catches your eye—or
another part of you—find a way to meet him and
start a conversation.

Rule: Don't shortchange yourself. If you're going to ask
him out, don't start with "I don't suppose you would
want to . . ." or "I know you'll say no, but how
about . . ." This gives the guy every reason in the
world to think there's some reason why he shouldn't
go out with you.

Rule: Don't sound like you're on a TV soap by saying
things like "Go out with me and you'll never regret
it" or "Let me take you out. It will be a night to
remember." Of course, if that works, you deserve
each other.

Rule: If he says no (or any variation: "I'm busy," "I've got
friends coming into town," "My mother is sick"),
continue to be pleasant. What's "no" today could be
"yes" tomorrow.

Rule: Never ask someone out while he's on a date with
someone else. Never ask someone out while you're
on a date with someone else.

"*Politeness is the art of choosing among one's real thoughts.*"

—ABEL STEVENS

Saying No

"Invariably a man will start talking to me," said Andrew, "and then suggest dinner or a drink. In one case it was a friend of a friend who asked me out and I said yes even though I didn't want to go. I feel badly saying no. I know a guy who, when he's asked out and isn't really interested, says, 'Sure, as long as you know it's a platonic thing.' I think that's worse. If I'm not interested, should I just cut him off before he has a chance to ask? Should I lie and say I have a boyfriend?"

Why is it never a matter of just saying no? For many, the delicate problem of rejecting a man's invitation is like rocket science: perplexing, alien, and beyond imagination.

Rule: Taking chances means that some conversations and some guys will turn out to be duds. If that happens, it's perfectly fine to say "no thanks" to an invitation and continue on with the conversation. Whatever you do, don't lie. Lies beget more lies and more complex lies.

Rule: If you're accepting an invitation with a caveat, be direct and honest about that. If it seems appropriate, let him withdraw the invitation. If a guy is rude or abusive after you've turned him down, tell him he's not only over, but over the line, and leave.

The Rules of the Dating Game

Gay dating, never an easy game, is now more complicated than ever. Take Jeremy's dilemma: "Clint and I had been kissing for nearly half an hour when I felt his hand reach for my belt buckle," said Jeremy. "Enjoying the sensation, I let him continue for a while before placing my hand on his, saying, 'Let's talk about this.' What ensued was a conversation about whether we should have sex on our second date. I told him that I was enjoying getting to know him and wanted to see more of him, adding, 'But I don't want to shortcircuit the future by jumping into bed too soon.' He agreed, and while flashing his big toothy smile at me, said, 'I wanna date you, too.' We agreed to wait before having sex."

Does waiting for sex ensure a more secure and long-lasting relationship? Do gay men have certain relationship problems because the rules are so ill-defined? What effect does being in the closet have on our ability to communicate, trust, and have relationships? And how has AIDS affected the dating lives of gay men? Those are some of the "big picture" questions. Then, of course, there are the day-to-day conundrums: "Should I call him or should I let him call me?" "How far should I go?" "When do we become 'boyfriends'?" "How out is he?" "How out am I?" "When is it okay to say 'I love you?'"

Lest you forget: Dating is supposed to be fun.

Rule: *Give at least three days' notice when asking a guy out. First dates are better scheduled on a weekday evening than on a Friday or Saturday—expectations are lower and each of you has an easy excuse to call the end of the evening early.*

Rule: Do things that you both enjoy; dating is about both of you. Be sensitive to his financial situation and budget (be sensitive to yours too!).

Rule: If you're seeing other people, be open and honest with him. Expect the same in return.

Rule: Don't try to remake him. If you don't like his friends, his fashion sense (or lack of it), his taste in music, or his haircut, he's probably not the right guy for you. Appreciate him for who he is. Conversely, don't let him try to change you. It'll never work. Note: You can attempt to change specific behaviors with varying degrees of success. For instance, is he always late? Does he forget to shave under his chin? Does he leave the milk out?

Rule: Demonstrate that you appreciate him without going overboard. Be generous with compliments, but limit gifts to holidays, birthdays, and anniversaries (no gifts for your "third week" anniversary).

Rule: Go slow and keep your expectations in check. There is no quicker way to end a relationship than by rushing things.

Rule: Talk to him. Listen to him. Practice, practice, practice.

> ## *"Bore: a person who talks when you wish him to listen."*
>
> —AMBROSE BIERCE

How to Turn First Dates into Second Dates

Are you a therapy graduate? Did your family win first prize in the "dysfunctional families sweepstake" last year? Do you have a child? Do you have a prison record? Are you a recovering alcoholic? While each of these examples is quite different, think through what and how much you want to disclose to a virtual stranger (and try to gauge his level of understanding), especially on a first date. It's one thing if you're in a café and he says, "I noticed you didn't drink any liquor tonight." If you wanted, you could say, "That's right, I'm in AA." However, to spend the evening talking about how crazy your family is may be offputting. Such disclosures early on can create distance rather than intimacy.

Timing is crucial.

Rule: Don't cry. Don't get angry. Don't get high or drunk. Don't gossip about mutual friends. Don't whine. Don't tell racist jokes. Don't talk about esoteric topics.

Rule: Never lie, but don't feel compelled to reveal your entire history and psyche to a new date (or friend). Take the time to build trust and confidence.

Rule: Don't ask for a second date before the first is over.

Making the First Move

Will is a successful restaurateur in Manhattan. At thirty-six, he's charming and intelligent. He dates infrequently, but tells friends he's still looking for the right guy. Enter Sean, a dashing architect who asks Will to dinner at his apartment. After a romantic candlelit supper, Sean invites Will to make himself comfortable in the room while he clears the table. "Put some music on," Sean calls as he passes from the kitchen to his bedroom. Will turns on the radio, which just happens to be preset to the "love songs" station. Suddenly, he feels Sean's hands on his back and turns to see his host wearing nothing more than a pair of silk boxers. "Hi," Sean whispers as he leans in to kiss Will. After a moment, Will says, "I'm not ready for this. Can we talk?" Ten minutes later, Sean is stroking Will's leg; Will breaks away and tells Sean he is leaving.

How do you read the signals? From the time we're teenagers, slyly and slowly putting our arms around that first date in the dark movie theater, we wonder what will happen. Will your date let it be, reciprocate, or go screaming out of the theater? When is it okay to touch? And where? To kiss? How deep? To go further? How far?

Rule: Don't assume because you're ready he is too. If in
     doubt, let him make the first move. If that takes too
     long (whether twenty minutes or sixteen dates), talk
     about it. Ask: "May I kiss you?" "May I hold you?"

Rule: Respect his wishes. Be clear about what you want.

Rule: Learn to interpret body language. People have dif-
     ferent signals to show they're attracted. A relaxed
     stance, open arms, a wide smile, grazing your arm,
     looking into your eyes mean one thing. Arms across
     the chest, a grimace, no eye or body contact, the
     maintenance of distinct space between the two of
     you means another. Got it?

"Charm is the ability to make someone else think that both of you are wonderful."

—EDGAR MAGNIN

When a Date Is Awful

Remember, no matter how miserable a date is, everyone survives. But how much do you have to endure in
the name of polite behavior? If he's a thumping bore,
embarrassing, a chain-smoker, or just generally unac-
ceptable, make an effort to see it through to the end.
However, if he's drunk or high, physically or verbally
abusive, or making unwanted sexual advances, by all

means beat it out of there. Even if he's paying, there'll be other free dinners.

Rule: *If someone's behavior is embarrassing or downright objectionable, tell him. If the verbal warning does not suffice, leave without making a big scene.*

Rule: *Don't be unnecessarily cruel. If your date hasn't been actually unpleasant, but you've had a crummy time just the same, thank him and either let him drop you home or take a cab. But if he wants to come in, tell him no. You've done your date duty. Say: "I had a nice time, but it's late. Goodnight."*

Rule: *Don't become a hostage to your answering machine, dreading that he will call and ask you out again. If he calls, talk to him and in your kindest and firmest voice say, "It's nice of you to ask, Dweezil, but I really don't think that's a good idea. It's nothing you did. I just don't think we have that much in common."*

The Right Way to Break a Date

Rex came rushing home from the university to get ready for his evening out with Rob. In high gear, he didn't see the flashing light on the answering machine until after he had showered, shaved, and put on his new linen shirt. "Rex, this is Rob. I'm sorry I can't make dinner tonight. Something's come up. Talk to you later." Said Rex, "The thing is he never called again. I understand that he may have had to cancel at the last minute, but I hate it when technology takes the place of talk. Let's face it: He was afraid to say it to my face."

Breaking a date is one of the most frequently mishandled social customs. The reason is twofold: People usually wait until the last moment and they're embarrassed by the time they do it. Treat your dates and potential dates with the same courtesy you do your friends and family (if you don't treat these people right, well, forget it).

Rule: *Don't make a date if you don't intend to follow through with it.*

Rule: *Give a person as much advance notice as possible if you are breaking a date.*

Rule: *If you have a legitimate excuse when breaking a date, give it. "Kurt, I'm sorry I can't go to the movies Friday, but my parents have decided to fly in from Spokane." If you're breaking a date because you've changed your mind entirely, be honest: "Jason, I don't think it's going to work out for us. Let's forget about dinner."*

Negotiating Safe Sex

The lights are down low. The votive candles flicker over the fireplace. Manny and Tim are settling in for a long winter's eve. With both men naked, Manny knows Tim's not wearing a condom. Tim purrs: "Just for a moment." Manny tenses and wonders to himself: "Is it too late to talk about safe sex now? Why didn't I talk about this before. What do I do now?"

Once upon a time it was okay to talk about a man's body being "to die for." Those days are long gone. In the Age of AIDS, the prevailing norm—the etiquette of our community—is safe sex (protecting yourself and protecting your partner). While a lot of guys are comfortable talking about sex, many get tongue-tied when it comes to simple declarative sentences like "I only do it safe" or "Here, put this condom on." Don't let embarrassment, fear of rejection, or the perception of diminished pleasure sway you from your course. Remember, if push comes to shove, here's a line that's worked for many: "Just what is it about *no* that you don't understand?"

The San Francisco AIDS Foundation recommends the following safe-sex guidelines:

- Always use condoms for anal and vaginal sex. Condom use does not guarantee protection from HIV, since condoms may break or be used improperly.
- Do not get semen, urine, feces, blood, or vaginal secretions in your mouth.
- Do not have mouth-to-rectum contact.

Rule: Call an AIDS hotline, talk to your doctor, or attend a safe-sex workshop and learn everything you can about safe sex and what you can do to end the epidemic. Learn how to put on a condom properly;

learn how to talk about safe sex; learn which sexual practices carry the greatest risk of HIV infection.

Rule: *Determine for yourself which behaviors you consider acceptable and which you don't. Stick to your guns—no matter how handsome he is, how sweet he is, how "negative" he says he is. Since safe sex means different things to different people, be sure to discuss each other's definition before engaging in sexual activity.*

Rule: *When using a condom, use only water-based lubricants that contain the spermicide nonoxynol-9 (this kills sperm). Oil-based lubricants—such as body lotions and Crisco—increase the likelihood of mechanical failure (the condom's breaking). Use only latex condoms; natural skin and lambskin do not provide protection from HIV. If your partner refuses to wear a condom, don't have sex with him.*

Rule: *Drugs and alcohol may impair your judgment and your resolve regarding safe sex. Use them sparingly.*

Playing the Field

Lowell's a "man's man" and he knows it. It's not uncommon for him to be dating two or three men simultaneously. While he takes extraordinary precautions to keep his lives separate (one boyfriend is upstate, another's a flight attendant, a third works the graveyard shift) and his sheets clean, it's not easy. "One evening as I was about to start making love to Ron—who had been on a trip to Tokyo for a week—I saw him look down at the floor, and there was a condom I had used the night before. 'Oh, jeez,' I said to myself." Ron responded immediately, "Why don't you throw that trash away?" as he began getting ready to leave.

People used to say that a smart man was one who knew how to play the field. Obviously, while a potentially entertaining option, it has its drawbacks. How much to tell? How do you handle introductions? What do you do with the evidence? The answers to these questions have everything to do with one word: monogamy. If you're in a mutually defined monogamous relationship and you're out playing the field, you're in big trouble. If you've agreed to date other people, then you need to negotiate with your partner(s) about just how much information to share. Perhaps one partner wants to know all the details, while another can live without them.

Rule: *Make rules that you can live with. You make manageable rules by talking with your partner about what each of you needs. Don't create rules for the kind of relationship you'd like to have, but for the kind of man you are and the relationship you're in.*

Rule: *If you have more than one suitor, don't share the confidences of one partner with the other. Don't play one guy against the other. Don't talk too much about the other.*

LOVE

Courtship and Romance

Years ago, Amy Vanderbilt described the long and necessary courtship that should occur before commitment: "The courtship period is casual and informal, without pledges on either side. It gives each a chance to know each other better—and yet make a graceful exit if it seems expedient. Each should give the other an opportunity to expose to searching consideration his best and worst sides. They should see each other in the give and take of family life, or at least among friends with kindred interests. Otherwise, a resulting marriage is in for rude shocks and accusations: 'If I'd known such-and-such I'd never have married you!'"

Unfortunately, many gay men hardly get to know a guy before settling into a relationship. Instant intimacy. Holiday honeys. Boyfriend *du jour*. Slow down, gents, you move too fast. The truth is a lot of men want to be courted, and there are a lot of men out there ready to go a-courtin'. Courtship means different things to different people and different couples, but for those of you seeking a "significant other" who lasts more than one season, read on.

Rule: Make sure he's available for the kind of relationship you want. When in doubt, ask.

Rule: Remember, pace and patience. Take your time getting to know him and allow him the time to get to know you. A little mystery is exciting.

Rule: Seek out men who are also looking to build a long-term relationship. The clearer you are about what you want, the more likely you are to achieve it.

Rule: Agree to hold off on having sex. Waiting until you feel more than lust has the potential to enhance your lovemaking. In a world often described as a supermarket of sex, a lot of men will appreciate that you're not "fast food."

Rule: Do special things for him. Bring him coffee in bed, tell him he's handsome, buy some attractive writing paper and use it, plan wildly romantic dates. Let it be fun. Don't cheat yourself—or him—out of romance.

Rule: Don't rush commitment. It takes time to know it's the right time to commit.

"The first sigh of love is the last of wisdom."

—ANTOINE BRET

The Right Time to Say "I Love You"

John, a handsome, well-built corporate muckety-muck, and Matthew, a publicist for a major arts organization, met at a political fundraiser. "It was like the

Fourth of July, Bastille Day, and my birthday all in one," recalls Matthew. "By the end of the first week John had asked me to go steady. I said yes. Two days later—nine days after we met—John turned to me one morning and said the three most beautiful words in the English language: 'I love you.' Although I've probably uttered those words to only two other men—after much longer courtships—I reciprocated. By the end of the month, he asked me to move in and travel less for my work. That's when I knew we were a train wreck waiting to happen—too fast, too soon."

Some people say "I love you" as though they were asking you to pass the salt. For others, it is a sacred phrase to be used sparingly, and with great meaning. Meanwhile, others think they hold the latter view but sprinkle it over any man who spends more than two nights. Remember: Words have value. Emotions have value. Love takes time.

Rule: The first time you want to say "I love you" to your new friend, don't. Think about what that pithy phrase really means to you and what it may mean to him.

The Right Answer to "Do You Love Me?"

"Evan, I love you," Jacques declared. "Do you love me?" "The words rang through my head like a drumbeat," said Evan. "Love? Sure, I like Jacques a lot, he's a great cook, a wonderful companion, and an attentive lover. But love?" What could he say? "Well, umm,

Jacques, let me think about it." Or "I'm not sure." Or should he lie and say, "Yes, of course." In the end he said, "I care for you very much, but I'm just not ready to say love yet. Do you understand?"

A premature admission of love can be embarrassing for both parties. If someone is brave enough to be honest with you about his feelings, respond with honesty.

Rule: Just because he says it to you (and presumably feels it), don't feel the need to reciprocate unless you feel the same way.

Rule: Don't avoid the question by kissing him or taking him to bed. Once asked, the question needs answering.

Valentine's Day

Is this a real holiday or a Hallmark holiday? Ask ten gay men and you're likely to get a fifty-fifty split. If you're a true believer, this is the one day when you want to make that special person in your life feel especially valued and loved (but, of course, they should feel that every day, right?). In the best of worlds, true believers match themselves with other true believers. But that's not always the case. In the event that a nonbeliever is paired with a true believer, the nonbeliever should try to meet the standard of his partner (or, at the least, agree to biennial celebrations of the holiday). True believers with discordant partners must remember that love does not have a price and that Valentine's Day is no litmus test.

Appropriate (and Inappropriate) Ways to Show You Care

Recently broken up with his lover of five years, Hal began dating "just the perfect man" soon after. With their romance going strong, he began showering Webster with all sorts of gifts. At first, it was the occasional bunch of flowers, then a nice tie, followed up with a matching shirt. A month into the relationship, Hal bought a color television for his boyfriend, who, it has to be said, loved all the attention and the gifts. The only problem for Hal: Webster wasn't reciprocating. Wondered Hal: "Was this love for sale?"

Gift giving can be a high-risk venture. Does it say too much (say, a color TV after a month)? Does it say enough (a paperback novel after a year)? Will he like it (will he tell you)? Can he return it (how will you feel)? Is there a hidden message attached (say, like a gym membership)? For some people gifts are an important way of expressing their affection. Others could care less.

Rule: Think carefully about your intended and your intended gift. Think about the potential message of a gift, whether positive or negative. Give gifts that are measured to the depth and intensity of your relationship.

Rule: Do not equate a material gift with love and security. Although often confused, gifts are not the currency of love.

Rule: A gift with a hidden agenda is no longer a gift.

Rule: Forget ESP. No one can read another's mind. If you want a particular gift, feel free to ask. He may or may not oblige you.

Rule: Regardless of the gift, tell him "Thank you."

SEX

One-Night Stands

One-night stands, or what's often called tricking, can be a satisfying way to have sex if both people agree that's what the tryst is about. You run into trouble only when one of you thinks it's a one-night stand and the other is convinced it's a first date. How do you avoid this problem? Unless you're having sex at a club or a backroom (where it should be pretty clear this is sex and not foreplay to dinner), you can't very well announce as you disrobe him, "I only want to have sex with you." But you might try, "I need to be in bed/back at the office/at my boyfriend's in an hour." It's certainly direct and makes the point. So does getting out of bed once you're finished or asking him to leave.

Rule: If it's a one-night stand, don't expect to exchange phone numbers—or even last names. When sex is just sex, etiquette adapts accordingly.

Rule: Remember to take all your personal belongings with you. You may never see him again; you certainly may never see the inside of his apartment again.

Phone Sex

The phone rings at 2 A.M. Who could that be? François wonders. "Who is that?" asks his lover. François picks it up. "Hey, this is Buck. I got your number on the chat line the other night. Wanna talk?" "Sorry," François says, "you must have the wrong number," as he sweats it out. Trying to fall asleep, François wonders how many other guys got his number that night. Will they call in the middle of dinner? What happens if his lover answers the phone?

There's no question, phone sex is 100 percent safe sex, and a widely practiced alternative in the Age of AIDS. There are two basic kinds of phone sex. The first type is with a for-pay virtual partner (basically a telephonic hustler). You tell him your fantasy; he plays it out with you. While often costly, it can usually be charged on a major credit card. The other kind is a chat line, which men call and are sequentially connected. These services often allow callers to choose from a menu that includes a private conference, group talk, J/O, S/M, bisexuality, muscle men, and those seeking real-life dates. This kind of service is less expensive, but can still add up.

Rule: Be cautious about giving your phone number on a group chat line; you may get calls at all hours.

Rule: Be sensible. Limit your time on these services so you won't be facing huge telephone bills. Shop around, read the fine print. Know what you're getting and what it will cost.

Rule: Fantasies are great over the phone, but if you do get together with a guy, always play it safe. If you intend to meet someone from the phone service, be accurate in how you describe yourself. If he really only wants blonds, you had better be a blond (a bottled "true" blond is fine, however).

Sex Clubs

There's no real mystery to what a sex club is all about. Still, there are some ground rules that will, no doubt, enhance your pleasure. Sex clubs, porn theaters, and so-called health clubs have existed in one form or another throughout the ages. Since the beginning of the AIDS epidemic, the climate in these clubs has changed dramatically—with a general push to greater health and safety practices (including the regulation of sexual activity and the distribution of safe-sex information and condoms). Most establishments don't allow high-risk sex (anal penetration), and many places now employ monitors, who make certain that patrons follow the rules.

Rule: No talking. No introductions. Show your interest in a man by approaching him and touching him. If you're approached by a guy you're not interested in, move away. If he persists, grasp his hand firmly and move it away.

Rule: If others attempt to join you and your partner—and that's not your thing—move the intruding hand or hands away. If it is, enjoy.

Rule: Wear clothing that's easy to pull on and off. Wear shoes that you won't mind getting dirty and wet.

Rule: If you see others engaging in unsafe sex, report the incident to a monitor and let him handle it.

Rule: If you see someone you know from the "outside," no greeting or introduction is necessary. A nod or a touch on the arm is appropriate, but again not required. Similarly, don't expect that because you've had sex with someone in a club he should acknowledge you on the outside. He needn't; nor should you. Note: After stand-up sex at sex clubs, romances have been known to start. If your heart speaks to you, break the rules. Tell him, "You were really super. Do you want to have a soda? Can I give you my number?"

"Every man has his price."

—Sir Robert Walpole

The Paid Escort

The subject of paid escorts is a tricky one because it is, quite honestly, an industry without quality or price controls. Individual escorts tend to have their own sets of rules and manner of conducting business. Escort services—located in all major metropolitan areas—are just as inconsistent. Bar hustlers, meanwhile, are the "freelancers" of the nether world of sex.

Your first consideration in engaging a paid escort is, without question, safety. Generally, escorts who run classified advertisements in the gay newspapers are considered the safest choice because their faces are known and their reputations established. Your risk is also diminished by using an escort service. A street hustler is another thing; he may be legitimate or he may be planning on rolling you or bashing you. Caveat emptor. Don't use your sex organ for a brain.

Rule: Always take precautions. If you decide to go with a bar hustler, ask the bartender if he knows the guy. When leaving the bar, be sure to say goodnight to friends and the bartender. If the hustler thinks peo-

ple will remember him, he's less likely to take advantage of you. If you're picking up a street hustler, the risk is much greater. Use common sense! A final safety precaution: Always have a supply of condoms with you.

Rule: Look carefully at the advertisements (and the pictures) and choose the guy who best fits your expectations. As with all products, remember, ads can be deceptive. When you call, tell him what you are looking for sexually (don't be embarrassed; he's heard it all and more), establish the price, the amount of time, and the location. Most escorts prefer to come to you (this is known as "out" as opposed to "in"). They usually charge slightly more for this service (transportation time and all that).

Rule: Be prepared to pay up front—in cash. Some escorts will wait until afterward to collect and may accept traveler's checks or personal checks (more likely if you're a regular). Some escort services accept credit cards, but you'll want to ask how the charge will appear on your billing statement. If you've enjoyed the service, a tip of 15 to 20 percent is customary.

Rule: If the escort arrives and is (a) unclean, (b) under the influence, or (c) has misrepresented himself in an important material way, you may refuse him, and his fee is forfeited.

Three-Ways

Lonnie and Mack decided several years ago to open up their relationship to include three-ways with guys they both found attractive. "This was *our* answer to having greater sexual variety without having sex outside the relationship. After five years together, we were still in love, but wanted different and hotter sex. It had all become too rote," says Mack. "We talked about how we would meet men—primarily at bars or through the personal ads. We also established some guidelines. First, safe sex at all times. Second, there were certain sexual acts that we would do between us but not with the third guy. The only real problem we've encountered is one of our regular 'partners' became really infatuated with Lonnie. We had to stop seeing him."

Rule: If you decide to open up your relationship to include others, be sure you're agreed. Don't pressure a reluctant partner.

Rule: Define the limits of your involvements. Develop a code between yourselves that allows the two of you to communicate while in bed with a third guy.

Rule: If you're the third party, be clear about your expectations—both with yourself and your prospective partners. Think about and talk through these issues beforehand.

> ## "Rudeness is the weak man's imitation of strength."
>
> —ERIC HOFFER

After-Sex Talk

You've just done *it*. Now what? And what do you say? "That was great!" "That was the best!" Or "Gotta go." Even if you're not a talker, a short conversation goes a long way to affirm the intimate experience you've just shared. Also, what you say next will determine how the rest of the evening goes. More than anything, it should be clear. "Would you like to spend the night?" Or "I'm really glad you came over, but I have to be up in the morning."

What if the sex wasn't good? Do you tell him? How? When? Criticism during sex is really out of the question (although a helping hand never hurts). If this is a guy you hope to see again, talk to him *later* about potential trouble spots. Be direct: "I like it this way." "That doesn't turn me on." "That hurt." Intimacy often softens hard truths. However, if you never intend to see the guy again, there's no point in giving him pointers.

Rule: Be clear in your communication about what you want. "Stay." "Go." "Come again." Be honest. Be direct.

"Two Cape Cods," Douglas tells the bartender, ordering the second for his new friend Jon. Douglas examines Jon more closely as they talk. He thinks: *Great body, sweet smile, a real nice guy.* After a few minutes and a brief discussion about jobs, neighborhoods, favorite restaurants, Jon asks Douglas: "So what do you like to do?"

"I love to roller blade, swim, hike, and I—"

"No, no," Jon interjects. "I mean, what do you do in bed?"

Douglas swallows hard. "You know, the regular things."

To many, this question—no matter how often asked—always seems unexpected and unsettling. What kind of answer is he looking for? What kind of answer are you comfortable giving? Is the answer always the same? Presumably, the literal intent of the question is: Are you top or bottom, Greek (active or passive), oral (active or passive), into S/M, drag, leather, diapers . . . you name it.

Answer honestly. If the time and place aren't right for this discussion, say so. If the question surprises you, tell him that. If you haven't decided to have sex with him, let him know that. If you're unsure about what kind of sex you might want with him, feel him out a bit. "Sometimes I like to let my partner take the lead. Other times I like to lead. Kissing is always very important to me. What do you like?" If you know what you want, tell the guy.

No matter how you respond, now is a good time to say, "Whatever goes, I do it 100 percent safely 100 percent of the time."

THREE

COMMITTED RELATIONSHIPS

We are all born for love. . . . It is the principle of existence and its only end.

—BENJAMIN DISRAELI

he day was rainy and gray as the two grooms finished dressing (each in a dark suit). For months the couple had been planning the wedding: everything from invitations and rings to seating charts, the right appetizers, wine, and champagne. And then, of course, there were the ceremony and the vows to be considered. Says Tom: "A gay man getting married has so many things to worry about. Even the small things assume hidden meanings and are riddled with symbolism." And why is he *marrying* Walter? "I'll show you what really got me thinking about marriage. Several months ago, this really wonderful photographer shot me and Walter. The picture got me thinking about appearances—the importance of declaring our commitment before people we love."

Without a doubt, traditional manners books make the wedding chapters the centerpiece of the tome: the be-all and end-all of civilized life. Certainly for gay men the questions are more complex and difficult because the community's institutions, mores, and customs are less formalized than their heterosexual counterparts. This chapter takes you step by step (but go in any order you please) from "Living Together" to "Formalizing Your Relationship" to "Troubled Times" to "When Baby Makes Three." As Harvey Fierstein, the noted playwright, once said: "Gay liberation should not be a license to be a perpetual adolescent. If you deny yourself commitment, then what can you do with your life?"

LIVING TOGETHER

Sharing an Address

Charley and David are finally living together—at David's place. It's taken them months of negotiations: Whose apartment? Whose furniture? Whose friends? "This was the first time for both of us," Charley says, "and we were both quite anxious about all the details. After the first three nights—and we argued every one of them—I remember thinking: 'Okay, been there, done that. I'm ready to go home.' It took time to resolve a lot of our issues. I'd be lying if I said that we'd wrapped that up. Living together—while truly wonderful—constantly poses its challenges."

These challenges are more the norm than the exception when a gay couple start to live together. Why is it that nothing seems more difficult than two men learning the art of compromise and how to talk to each other?

Rule: If your partner is moving into your house, make room for him. Give up half your closet space and your drawers. Think about new ways to arrange the furniture, and, yes, you must find space for that portrait of his mother.

Rule: *Talk about and agree to a household budget from the get go. Because there are no specific "roles" in a gay household, all tasks are up for grabs (who does the marketing, cleaning, clothes washing, and gardening). Divide tasks by interest, skill, and time available.*

Rule: *Don't open his mail (unless he specifically asks you to). Respect his privacy. Treat your partner as an equal.*

Rule: *Be sensitive to the fact that some family members may disapprove of your living together, but do not allow them to show disrespect to your partner. Explain to your family that he is your family.*

"*Arguments out of a pretty mouth are unaswerable.*"

—JOSEPH ADDISON

Together, Forever? Photos of Past Lovers

That first evening after Kip moved into Spencer's house, he noticed Spencer still had the photos of his two previous lovers on the dresser in *their* bedroom. "It didn't really bother me before, but now that it's our room, I don't want his former husbands looking down on us," Kip said. When he asked Spencer about removing the pictures, he was surprised by his response: "They're my friends. That's all. But they're still a part of my life." What to do?

Moving in together signals a new beginning. It can be manifested by new sheets, new towels, new underwear, but above all by a new attitude. The notion of "ours" must be introduced into the relationship and the household—and fast.

Rule: Pictures of past lovers, boyfriends, even wives have no place in the new couple's bedroom, which is not to say the offending photos can't be moved to a study or an out-of-the-way bookcase. Supposedly you have made a commitment to your new partner and to him alone.

Caveat: Photos and other mementoes of deceased lovers are permissible anywhere in the new household. A healthy relationship should not be threatened by the dead (of course, a healthy relationship should not be threatened by the past, either). The dead should be remembered and honored as best we can.

Making the News Public

Two gay men living together—who are not in college or twentysomething bachelors—are increasingly common in the major urban centers of this country. Many cities now recognize these relationships and provide recognition of them through "domestic partnerships." This is a serious form of commitment—one that should be taken seriously by gays and straights alike.

Rule: *Upon moving in together, send change-of-address cards that include both your names and your new address to both sets of friends and family members. Throw a housewarming to celebrate not only your new home but your relationship.*

Rule: *Invitations should now be addressed to both of you and, generally, accepted by both. Sometimes it takes a while to educate friends (both gay and straight) that you expect to be invited as a couple to various functions. If one of you is left off an invitation, call and say: "Bill and I are now settled in this great town house in the Palisades. We're really looking forward to having you and Marge over for dinner soon." Hopefully, that will prompt Marge's lover to say, "Oh my, I didn't realize you and Bill were living together. We hope he can come on the fourteenth?" Most people try to do the right thing and make their friends comfortable.*

Rule: *If you live in a city where you are eligible to become domestic partners, find out more about that process and talk with your partner about doing it (if of interest).*

Sharing a Bathroom

In the best of all worlds, you'd have a two-bath house. In the next-best scenario, you have adjacent sinks and lots of mirror space. How many fights have started in the bathroom? "You take too much time." "What could you possibly be doing in there and still look like that?" "You used up all the toothpaste/shampoo/contact lens solution/toilet paper again!" If you have only one bathroom (like most of us), make consideration of your partner a priority. Gone are the days when your towels landed in a soggy heap on the floor, when you never put the toothpaste cap back on, and when you cleaned the bathtub "whenever." It's also not a bad idea to find that special place for sex toys and other paraphernalia; you never know when his or your Aunt Elizabeth will come visit.

Rule: Invest in a hamper and use it.

Rule: If you use the last of something, replace it before "next week."

Rule: A closed door is a closed door—particularly when it's the bathroom door. Always knock. Always listen to his answer. Even though you're a couple now, you may not want to share everything!

"It destroys one's nerves to be amiable every day to the same human being."

—Benjamin Disraeli

When His Cute Habits Turn Annoying

You've been living together for a while and suddenly you realize things have changed. Before, it didn't matter that he never recycled, never picked up the dry cleaning, never took out the garbage, put the toilet paper on the roll backward . . . well, we could keep going until the millennium. What to do? You need to address these concerns in a constructive manner. Realize that his habits were long in the forming and, no doubt, they'll be long in the undoing. And don't forget that your "cute" habits are, for sure, just as annoying to him.

Rule: Make compromise a significant building block of your relationship. Compromise will play a big part in resolving these dilemmas. Does it matter that you always forget to turn off the VCR? Does it matter that he never makes the bed?

Rule: Just because you've "always done it that way" or "it never bothered anyone before" doesn't make it right. That was then, this is now. Change is good and an integral part of any healthy relationship. But be patient: No one, not even you, can change overnight.

FORMALIZING YOUR RELATIONSHIP

Ceremonies of Commitment

In midafternoon on that rainy Saturday, Tom and Walter stood up in front of seventy friends, family members, and colleagues. They drank champagne and then, facing each other, exchanged their vows: "I commit to you my life and my love for the rest of our days." Then, like couples everywhere, they put on their gold bands and kissed each other. A few moments later, Tom's brother made a toast: "Tom and Walter have done something gay people have dreamed of for thousands of years. Let's raise our glasses to Tom and Walter. May you continue your life together in a more perfect union, in good health, and always with adventure and purpose and love."

These events are called "unions," "affirmation ceremonies," "ceremonies of commitment," "life partnership ceremonies," a "blessing of love," a "rite of blessing," a "covenant of love," and, of course, "weddings." Whatever you decide to call your ceremony, it's clearly an expression of your love and commitment to each other. It's also a way to formalize and make public your commitment to each other in front of your friends and family (and possibly to printers, florists, caterers, photographers, and musicians). It may, in fact, be the ultimate "coming out" event. (In the following pages, the words "wedding" and "marriage" have been used for convenience and consistency; always use language and terms that reflect your values and sentiments.)

Who Pays for What?

As relatively uncharted territory for gay men, general rules for gay weddings haven't been formalized. Most couples accept equal responsibility for expenses (depending on ability to pay), while others gladly receive cash and in-kind assistance from friends and family members. James and Andy explained how they paid for their ceremony: "We decided to have a small wedding and pay for it ourselves, although we had both dreamed of something grand. After we began talking about our plans, some remarkable things happened. James's mother said that she would give us $5,000 either toward the ceremony or as a wedding gift, because that's what she had given James's sister. My best friend offered us his house on the bay and said he would take care of the liquor bill. We were already reeling in disbelief when another friend, a baker, said she would make us the 'best wedding cake ever.' Everyone's efforts allowed us to afford the most beautiful day and have a honeymoon in Bermuda. It was just an incredible outpouring of love."

Rule: Start saving. Talk about how much the ceremony (and all the other add-ons, like rings, invitations, gifts for members of the wedding party) will cost. Make a budget and do your absolute best to keep to it. The measure of the day is not in the dollars spent.

Rule: If friends or family members offer to assist (and there are no burdensome strings attached), be gracious and accept their offers.

Fashion Advice for Two Grooms

Larry and Gil had very different ideas about dressing for their special day. "Larry had decided that since we were having the ceremony outdoors we should go casual. I disagreed. Outdoors, yes. Picnic, no. This was a once-in-a-lifetime event. Actually, I wanted us to go the whole nine yards, with both of us wearing English morning suits. Larry thought I was being pompous and unnecessarily fussy. After weeks of bickering, we agreed on vintage clothing. Larry settled on a dark gray pinstripe suit from the thirties, and I chose a Casablanca-style shawl-collar dinner jacket and black slacks from the fifties. Our friends thought it was such a great way to go that a lot of them came in vintage wear, too."

One of the great things about "getting hitched" is the romance and fantasy (however you define such things). While your basic black tuxedo is the standard for truly formal events, express yourself sartorially however you wish. As in everything else about this day, keep to a theme.

Rule: If you choose to go formal, wear the traditional tuxedo, a cutaway or morning coat, or a stylish dinner jacket and black slacks (see "Formal Attire," p. 167, for more). If you will be renting tuxes for a large group, get a discount.

Rule: Military uniforms (if you served), ethnic costumes, or dark suits are good alternatives to traditional wedding clothes.

Rule: Whatever you wear, photographs of it will go down for posterity. Look ahead ten years and ask yourself: "Do I want to be seen wearing that outfit?"

> *"Love does not begin and end the way we seem to think it does. Love is a battle, love is a war, love is a growing up."*
>
> —JAMES BALDWIN

The Ceremony

Do you want to be married on a hilltop at sunset? At high noon on the beach? At your club? Your parents' house? In church? In the afternoon? Cocktail hour? Evening? Create a ceremony that best suits the two of you, your relationship, and your expectations for the day. Tradition does not weigh down heavily on two gay men forming a union as it does for many heterosexual couples; in fact, there really is none. You have the opportunity to fashion new traditions. But whatever else you do that day, the ceremony is the linchpin of the wedding and should be reflective of your love, commitment, and faith.

Most ceremonies include the following parts:

- An introduction (any kind of opening remarks, a processional, a musical interlude)
- The main body (for instance, prayers, readings, testimonials)
- The vows
- The ring ceremony

- A pronouncement (if you've changed your names, the new names are announced here as well as a statement that parallels "I now pronounce you husband and wife")
- The closing (this almost always includes the kiss, another musical interlude, and the recessional)

"Unto you is paradise opened."

—1 Esdras 8

The Vows

Your vows are the core of the ceremony, the heart of the matter. Many people consider their vows to be the most important part of any ceremony. And what is a vow? It is a promise or promises (in essence a verbal contract) to your partner and should define the basis of your relationship and your love. Vows should be simple, eloquent, and heartfelt.

Rule: Prepare your vows. Do not speak extemporaneously. Above all, speak from your heart. If you are nervous, it is perfectly acceptable to read from a small piece of paper during the ceremony.

Rule: If you find a reading or a poem that captures your sentiments and love, incorporate it into your vows (giving credit where credit is due).

Rule: Vows may be humorous, flowery, or serious. Try not to use too many metaphors ("You are a lightning rod in the rainstorm of life"). Keep vows brief (we're sure you could recite volumes about your beloved, but save it for the honeymoon).

Rule: The word "obey" is no longer appropriate vow-speak. Use "cherish" instead.

The Guest List

After five years of living together, Noah and Richard decide they want to get "married." They want the official sanction of a legal domestic partnership and the recognition from their families and friends. Neither set of parents is pleased about this latest wrinkle in their relationship. In particular, Richard's homophobic Aunt Alice is threatening to boycott the ceremony. Neither Noah nor Richard wants to invite Alice, although Richard's mother is insistent that her sister be invited. They ask: "Do we have to?"

No. Only those who can fully honor and love the couple to be joined are asked to be in attendance. That's it. Homophobia is a social error of the highest magnitude. It is not rewarded with party or wedding invitations.

Rule: Don't invite friends or relatives you won't be comfortable to have sharing the day. Don't invite people expecting they won't come (they might). Don't invite people hoping for a great present (you may not get one). Don't not invite people assuming they'll be uncomfortable (let them decide).

Rule: Don't invite more people than you can afford. Keep to your budget.

The Invitation

There are many ways to approach the invitation—in terms of both style and content. In truly formal invitations, you will find a complex "wedding ensemble," consisting of the ceremony invitation, the reception invitation, the response card, an outer envelope, an inner envelope, and a self-addressed envelope. Most etiquette books have devoted entire chapters to the intricacies of the wedding invitation, and the Resources section on page 213 is an additional source for books with these details.

Here are two variants on a gay wedding invitation. Feel free to adapt these forms as you see fit, making sure that your guests can extract what they need. Most important: the date, the time, and the place.

Let this be our destiny—

To love, to live,

To begin each new day together,

To share our lives together.

Rodney Lynn Jackson

and

Robert Clark Paris

Will be joined in marriage

On Saturday, the twenty-second of July,

Nineteen hundred and eighty-nine,

At eleven o'clock in the morning.

Unitarian Community Church

1260 Eighteenth Street

Santa Monica, California

Reverend Ernest D. Pipes, Jr.

Reception to follow

Less formal:

JAMES DESMOND WOODS

&

PAUL DAVID YOUNG

INVITE YOU TO CELEBRATE THEIR UNION

53 GANSEVOORT STREET

NEW YORK CITY

SATURDAY, NOVEMBER 5, 1994

6:30 COCKTAILS

8:00 DINNER

RSVP 555-2448

NO GIFTS, PLEASE

More than anything else the invitation sets the tone for the prospective ceremony. If you receive an invitation on heavy stock, expect a formal event. If it arrives via your e-mail address, look forward to something on the less traditional side.

Rule: The invitational lines often list the hosts of the wedding, whether they be the grooms, the grooms' parents, or the grooms' friends. It's perfectly acceptable

*for those not paying for the wedding to be listed
here if they support you.*

*Rule: Full names are used on invitations. Although brides'
names have traditionally preceded grooms', with
two grooms it makes sense to list names alphabetically.*

*Rule: Instead of "The honor of your presence is
requested," consider the following lines:*

- *. . . request the pleasure of your company*
- *Please join us . . .*
- *With joy and love James and Paul invite you to
  join them in the celebration of . . .*

*Rule: Spell out the date and the year. Spell out all words
(like "Street" and "Boulevard"), except Dr. and Jr.*

*Rule: The time of the ceremony and reception are writ-
ten out. If the reception is to be held in a different
location, include a separate reception invitation
card.*

Again, much of this information refers to a formal
invitation to a formal event. Feel free to purchase or
design invitations in line with the kind of ceremony you
have in mind. Many couples print their invitations on
their own home computers, make use of border cards (a
hefty-weight card with a preprinted border that can look
very smart), or even adapt postcards and preprinted invitations.

How to Address the Invitation

For general guidance on this, see "How to Address Envelopes to a Gay Couple," page 143. Here are some specific rules for wedding invitations.

Host Rule: Addresses should generally be handwritten (or done in calligraphy). Use black ink.

Host Rule: Try not to use the term "and Guest." If your good friend Joe Singleton has a main squeeze, take the trouble to find out his name and send him a separate invitation (modernists may choose to include him on Joe's invitation)—unless they live together (in which case we assume you know his lover's name), when, of course, they receive one invitation.

Host Rule: If you don't want children present, do not mention them on the invitation. If a guest asks to bring a child, respond either by explaining you're really not set up for that ("I don't know where little Jack would go") or that you really will have no room ("We're already at our limit").

Guest Rule: Only those whose names appear on the invitation are invited. Do not ask to bring a date, a family member, or even a visiting celebrity.

When Invitations Should Be Sent

Let's back up a bit. Once you've decided to have a commitment ceremony, take the time to do some real planning. This will pay off in spades.

Rule: About six months before the event, rough out your guest list and choose a date. Look at various cards and invitations. About three months before, start talking about the wording and style of invitations. Begin to finalize your invitation list. Tell family and friends to save the date—especially out-of-towners who will need to make reservations.

Rule: Two to three months before the big day, order the invitations. Finalize your list. Figure out a system of tracking RSVPs and gifts given.

Rule: Mail invitations four to six weeks before the event. Make sure you have the correct amount of postage applied (on both the outer envelope and the response-card envelope).

Choosing a Suitable Gift

If you're invited to a gay wedding, then (in addition to the RSVP) you have two obligations: to arrive on time (no gay time here, brothers) and to buy a gift for the couple that evidences thought and caring. Tradition stipulates that gifts be delivered either before the wedding or within one year (but not actually taken to the event because of the possibility of its being misplaced or the card and the box somehow becoming forever separated). If the couple has decided to register at a department store, or for a painting, or at a specialty boutique, the easiest and safest thing is to participate in the registry. By doing it this way, you ensure that your gift will be something they want—and not their fourteenth blender. Even if you don't choose a gift from the registry, check out what they have selected; it will give you a better idea of their tastes and needs.

A material wedding gift is but one expression of your caring and love for the couple. Other ways to show you care include throwing a bachelor or engagement party—even a shower, donating your services as a calligrapher, or lending your living room for the ceremony.

Rule: Traditional etiquette rules against cash as a wedding gift. Whether or not you follow this rule, the couple to be married should not ask for cash.

Rule: Some couples have decided to include a card within the invitation explaining that they would prefer their guest to make a donation to a specific charity rather than give a present. An example:

In lieu of gifts
please make a donation in honor of our wedding to
Continuum HIV Day Services
Ten United Nations Plaza, Suite 200
San Francisco, California 94102

Rule: Purchase returnable gifts if you are not using the registry. No couple needs six Cuisinarts, four microwaves, and twenty-two vases.

Rule: If you want to give a one-of-a-kind nonreturnable gift, be very, very careful. Be absolutely sure of their taste, their apartment, and their needs.

Répondez s'il vous plâit

"It was two weeks before our ceremony and I still hadn't heard 'yea' or 'nay' from one-third of my guests," exclaims Bart. "One-third! Everything—from the caterers to the table arrangements—was dependent on knowing who and how many were coming."

You bet. Nowadays, there is such a lax attitude about responding to invitations in general, and weddings in particular, that we hardly know what to say other than: *You absolutely must abide by the date given on the response card sent with your invitation.* (The deadline response will be about two weeks before the event.) No excuses. No changing your mind a day before (except for an extraordinary reason like a death in your immediate family or severe illness). If a blank card has been sent, write in your response (most formally: "Prescott Parberry accepts with pleasure Geoffrey Wilson and Marvin Pearlstein's invitation for Saturday, the sixth of May," or much more informally: "I'm so looking forward to sharing your wedding day with you. Love, Scotty.")

If a preprinted response card has been included in the invitation, fill in the blanks.

Rule: Make sure you have accepted or regretted before the deadline; otherwise you'll truly regret it.

The Reception

Think about weddings you've gone to. Sure, you remember the ceremony, but, if you're like most, it's the basics that count (and linger): the food, the flowers, the music, and the cake. As the couple getting married, you may never even taste your dinner—or hors d'oeuvres or whatever you decide to serve—but your guests most certainly will talk.

Rule: Get written contracts from all vendors (caterers, florists, musicians, etc.) whenever possible. Make them as specific as you can. This is the best possible guarantee that you'll be getting what you ordered— and will provide the best recourse if you don't.

THE SKINNY ON CATERERS: It's important to choose the right food service to match the tone and timing of your event—and to find a caterer who can do it well and at a reasonable cost. Go as simply or elaborately as you wish. In choosing the food and the caterer, think about the overall theme. For instance, if your attire is formal, you probably don't want an afternoon barbecue by the lake. A good caterer should help you decide on a theme and work out a budget.

How do you find a good caterer? *Experience and word-of-mouth.* Remember how great that meal was at Uncle Jack's retirement party? Isn't it time to call Aunt Vera and Uncle Jack? Talk to your friends, family, and coworkers. Good caterers tend to rise to the surface. If you've hired a photographer, he's probably eaten at as many of these events as Elizabeth Taylor. Ask him or her. Finally, is there a restaurant the two of you love? It's worth giving them a call. Or you may even want to hold the reception there.

Once you've found a caterer, here are some things to remember:

Rule: *If you're set on a particular theme or menu, don't let your caterer sell you on a "preset" menu of items he or she has purchased in volume (unless the savings are significant and important to you). It's your special day: part of the joy of it is making it unique.*

Rule: *Presentation and service are as important as the food. Discuss station setup, serving pieces, linens, and server attire. Most caterers have photographs of their other events. If they don't offer, ask to see them.*

Rule: *Costs are most often calculated on a per-guest basis. Find out exactly what that includes (and what it doesn't include), with a breakdown for specific charges. Get it in writing!*

Rule: *Be aware that bar costs can account for up to 45 percent of your catering bill. If you can, buy your own liquor, soda, and bottled water.*

Rule: *Be sure to get the name of the on-site contact person and, if possible, arrange to meet him or her ahead of time.*

Rule: Be sure that the caterer briefs all servers that this is
a gay reception. Tell him or her that if anyone is
uncomfortable he should keep it to himself or not
work your party.

THE NATURE OF FLOWERS: Wildflowers? Peonies? An
assortment of cabbage and tea roses? Flowers help add a
luxurious if not fragrant touch to complete a wedding
day. Be warned: They can be expensive. As with caterers,
word-of-mouth is the best indicator of a quality florist or
floral designer.

Rule: Decide what flowers you will want at the ceremony,
the reception, and any to be pinned to your lapel.
To keep your costs down, choose flowers that are in
season and locally grown (orchids from the
Philippines or tulips flown in from Holland can go
for a tidy sum). Use fewer flowers and more green-
ery in arrangements and centerpieces to extend your
flower budget and to camouflage work stations. Be
sure to discuss table placement with the caterers, so
they know what to expect when they set the table.

Rule: Men in wedding parties generally wear bouton-
nières in their left lapels. Traditionally, the groom's
boutonnière is based on the bride's bouquet. The
appropriate adaptation? A single flower such as a
red rose for each groom and different-color roses for
the other men in the wedding party look great.

> ## "Music is well said to be the speech of angels."
>
> —Thomas Carlyle

THE SOUND OF MUSIC: Whether you're planning a string quartet for the dinner hour, a disc jockey for dancing, or a strolling banjo picker, music adds life and warmth to any party. The music should be chosen in accordance with the kind of affair you are planning. If you intend to have dancing, do you want a live band or a disc jockey? Take the time to listen to several bands, disc jockeys, and other musicians, then make an informed choice.

Rule: Check out the noise restrictions for the location where your reception will be held. Also, ask your performer to do a test run at the site to see if there are any acoustical problems.

Rule: If you plan music, make sure it lasts as long as the reception does. When selecting music for the evening, consider your guest list. There should be something for everyone there—as well as your favorite songs.

Rule: Find out if your band or disc jockey can make a tape of the event for you. It will make a great keepsake.

TAKING THE CAKE: In the Broadway show that is your wedding, the cake is the grand finale. You are probably already conjuring up images of all those traditional four-tier white wedding cakes you've had the pleasure of enjoying. A cake is really memorable only if it is exceptionally good or exceptionally bad. Again, talk to your friends and family members for the names of good bakers.

Rule: Order your cake as far in advance as possible. Bakers book up quickly and well in advance of the date.

Rule: You can make your own same-sex cake topper from components available at your local craft store or buy a premade one through Shocking Grey, a specialty mail-order catalog.

PICTURE PERFECT: Hiring the right photographer (for stills and videos) is crucial to preserving memories of your ceremony and reception for years to come. If you're spending all this money for your special day, you'll want an equally special record of the day. Wedding photographers are very expensive, so expect to drop a little change here. Be sure to establish all costs up front and be completely clear on what your package includes.

Rule: Interview several photographers, since fees, packages, and talent vary greatly. Be sure to discuss candid photos as well as portraits.

Rule: Make sure that you'll get the opportunity to view your proofs and select which will become prints shortly after your wedding. Good wedding photographers usually take no fewer than 150 shots for you to choose from. Find out how long your photographer keeps the negatives, or if you can arrange to keep them.

Rule: Before the important day, talk with the photographer about shooting a same-sex wedding. Give the photographer a written list of those persons or shots that you want covered and have a friend act as a liaison, so you're sure he or she gets the shots.

Guest Rule: Be aware of the camcorder and its hidden microphone. Everything you say may be recorded for decades to come.

TROUBLED TIMES

When Unhappiness Abounds

It goes without saying that every couple will regularly argue, row, squabble, fight, and otherwise make life miserable for each other. Whether it's over a minor item ("You forgot to take the trash out again") or a major infraction ("How could you sleep with my best friend?"), it's important to stay calm, reason with the facts, keep focused on the issue, and listen to what your partner is saying.

Perspective is an important commodity to invest in. During an all-out assault, it can be difficult to remember that this "super rat" is the man you love. If possible, give yourselves a cooling-off period. At the very least, that time should take off some of the edge, with many couples finding that their troubles seem altogether less important later than now.

Rule: *Be clear about the issue at hand—even if that means repeating it over and over again. Many people pull extraneous issues into an argument (like their entire relationship history), which only make matters worse and more difficult to resolve.*

Rule: *Be sure of what you want to accomplish or gain as a result of the argument. There is no point in fighting for fighting's sake. Don't raise your voice at your partner. Keep swearing to a minimum. Both these tactics will serve only to escalate the situation.*

Rule: *Listen to him. Be open to seeing his point of view, even if you disagree with it. Try to turn a fight into a conversation that can be resolved through mutual compromise.*

Rule: *Don't fight to win. Neither of you will be satisfied. Remember, when one wins, two lose.*

Rule: *Don't argue while under the influence of alcohol or drugs.*

Rule: Never, under any circumstances, resort to physical confrontation. There is no excuse for domestic violence. If your partner is physically abusive, do not continue to talk with him. Leave.

"Don't take the wrong side of an argument just because your opponent has taken the right side."

—Baltasar Gracián

Breaking Up Is Hard to Do

"The plan was simple," stated Harlan. "Devon had agreed to come over at 2 P.M. We'd go for a walk and talk. He arrived right on time, wearing the sweater I had given him on our second anniversary. I was nervous about breaking up with him. Inside my head I told myself: *This is what you want. But you have to start the conversation.* Taking his arm in mine, I jumped off the proverbial cliff: 'Devon, I've got some things on my mind. While I understand you want to have sex with other men, I'm just not comfortable with that kind of arrangement after all this time.' I stammered some. Then Devon spoke up: 'I agree. I think wanting to make this an open relationship is my way of saying I'm not willing to stay committed in the ways we've discussed. I'm sorry.' We walked a little more and then headed back to the house. We hugged and said good-bye. A few days later we began talking about all the details of dissolving the relationship."

There's no smoothing over the rough edges of a breakup between two people who love each other. There will be pain, sadness, anger, loneliness, and, sometimes, the desire for revenge. Generally, breakups bring out the worst in us—and seem like an excuse to forget all manners and consideration. Although breakups leave the emotions dangling, it's important to act in as appropriate a manner as you can (whether you're deep-sixing him or the one being dumped).

Rule: If you're determined to break up (and you've exhausted all other remedies), do it and be done with it. Now is not the time to be wishy-washy or allow lines to blur. You'll have plenty of time to worry about a friendship down the road.

Rule: Be honest. He deserves the truth stated as plainly as you can. Don't say things like "It's just not working out." Tell him the specific reasons.

Rule: If you share a home, a car, a pet (and any other joint possessions), both parties have an obligation to work out a mutually satisfactory agreement. If that proves difficult—even after some time has passed— you might consult a professional mediator. Fiscal responsibility transcends the life of a relationship.

Rule: If you're the one who was left: Take care of yourself. Take charge of your life. Learn the lessons as soon as you can. *Don't romanticize the past. Try not to obsess. Move on.*

Announcing Your Breakup Publicly

Your friends will throw all the clichés at you: "He wasn't good enough for you." "Your next lover will be better." "You won't be celibate forever." "You're not getting older, you're getting better." And on and on. Still, if you're like most guys, you will feel wronged—especially if Mr. Wonderful, or rather Mr. Perfectly-Awful, has left to be with another man. It is important for both of you to handle the announcement and subsequent discussion as freely of malice and finger pointing as you possibly can (you get extra credit for trying).

Rule: Don't boast about dumping your lover. While close friends, family members, and trusted coworkers can be told the real reasons for the split, the larger world doesn't need any explanations. If you're dating a new man, that will be apparent soon enough.

Rule: If one of you intends to remain in your building, inform your landlord, superintendent, or doorman. The one staying on may also want to change the locks, depending on the nature of the breakup.

Rule: Don't try to turn social situations into occasions to seek votes for your side. There's nothing democratic about love or war.

Friends: Who Gets to Keep Whom?

Victor and Paul had been lovers for a decade when Victor left Paul for a younger man. Their friends found the divorce a messy thing, but more than that, they realized how difficult it is to stay true to two. Indeed, that's often the case. On the other hand, it's fairly rare that friends are equally attached to both partners. Taking a closer look at Victor and Paul's circle, it's easy to determine who actually initiated which friendships and who had closer ties to which friends. That's one way for them to decide (if this were the soon-to-be-ex-couple's decision, which, usually, it's not).

When lovers part, friends sometimes must choose (particularly if it's nasty). Often, two hateful exes actually make their friends choose one or the other. Of course, there will be crossovers; these friends must play their double billing with extreme care.

Rule: If you remain friends with both members of a defunct couple, do not trade in gossip between them. Appear 100 percent loyal to the one you're with.

Rule: If you're a member of a defunct couple, don't make your friends choose one or the other. If need be, set some rules, like never mentioning his name again. Be as reasonable as you can.

> *"In taking revenge a man is but equal to his enemy, but in passing it over he is his superior."*
>
> —FRANCIS BACON

A Word on Revenge

After Nathan discovered that Pete was cheating on him, and actually had been for several months, he threw him out of their apartment (but didn't actually change the locks). But Pete stayed on for another month—mostly while looking for a new place—coming and going as he pleased, lying to Nathan, and refusing to pay his share of the bills. Eventually he left, taking some of Nathan's belongings. Said Nathan: "I wanted to get back at Pete for all the lousy things he had done. In the heat of the moment, I purposely made a scene at his job in an attempt to get him fired. I was just so angry—and hurt—that one evening I broke the windshield on his truck." In no time, Pete had gotten a restraining order against Nathan, who—previously the victim of a deceitful lover—was now seen as a harassing and vengeful stalker.

Revenge is a natural emotion, particularly if you think you've been done wrong by your man. But how much better it is to fantasize your revenge than actually achieve it. In the end, a "successful" campaign of revenge has no winners.

Rule: Two wrongs do not make a right. Remember that! Say it over and over. If you're thinking of acting out, talk to a close friend about your plans.

Rule: You will have to live with the memory—and perhaps photographic, journalistic, or even criminal record—of your actions. Proceed with caution and, above all, a cool head.

Rule: Buy a voodoo doll. Write truly hateful letters—and then put them away. Seek a constructive way to work through your feelings.

WHEN BABY MAKES THREE

Announcing the Newest Member of Your Family

For heterosexuals, letting the world know of the birth of a child is old hat. What happens when a gay man or a gay couple have such an announcement? Actually, we have many of the same resources and avenues as our straight friends. You may hand out cigars at work, put a notice in your local newspaper, or, as most folks do, take pen to paper.

For those interested in the most formal presentation, visit a quality stationer who sells engraved cards. Obviously pink is traditional for little girls and blue for boys, but you might want to do something gender nonspecific here. In any case, the information is typically engraved in black with the baby's calling card attached to the larger announcement. A less expensive option is store-bought announcements, available at any stationery store.

Rule: The baby's birth announcement should contain the following information:

> *Baby's full name: Alexandra Morrison-Barrows*
>
> *Birth date: 12 July 1994*
>
> *Parents' names: Michael Morrison and Stanley Barrows*
>
> *Parents' address: 1234 Main Street, Provincetown, MA*

You may also include the time of birth, the name of the hospital, and the baby's birth weight. Note: It's always a good idea to personalize any announcement.

Rule: No discussion or announcement is necessary about how the baby was conceived or received. If a child is adopted as a baby, an announcement similar to the birth announcement can be sent. Something along these lines:

> Dean Harper and Paul Day
> are pleased to announce the arrival of their daughter
> Julia Harper-Day
> Born October 21, 1994
> Arrived January 6, 1995

> ### *"There is no friendship, no love, like that of the parent for the child."*
>
> —HENRY WARD BEECHER

Choosing the Baby's Last Name

Married heterosexual couples who do not share the same surname have been plagued by this dilemma for a couple of decades. What to call baby? Most heterosexuals decide to make life easiest for baby by giving it the father's surname. This is simply a matter of practicality, a decision that also reflects the patriarchal nature of society. With two fathers, life is more complicated.

Rule: In practical terms, it makes sense to give the baby the surname of the legal father (in most states only one individual can be a legal father). Of course, a hyphenated name may be used as well.

Rule: If you have more than one child, give all your children the same surname. It helps foster the right kind of family values.

"Out" in the Community

Leon and Tim have adopted two baby girls in the Los Angeles area. Leon says that "when I'm on the playground with Maria and Eliza, everyone we meet assumes I'm a heterosexual dad and that the kids' mom is at work or at home. I'm determined, both for my own self-respect and also for the children, to be out everywhere. Sometimes this means taking the initiative in a conversation. Last week, I was at the florist buying some hydrangeas and the clerk said, 'Oh, I'm sure your wife will love these.' I said, 'Actually, I'm sure my husband will.' It might have been easier to let the comment go, but I can't anymore."

Being gay and having a child adds a new dimension to being out. You are responsible not only for how you present yourself (and perhaps a partner) to the outside world, but for the image that you project to your child. In the best of worlds, a strong, positive image is always the goal. Still, there are other factors at play. Some people simply do not want to be gay rights advocates every time they go to the supermarket or the playground; it's challenging and often exhausting. Depending on where you live, it may be wiser to be less open about your parenting situation.

Rule: Talk with your partner in advance of potentially troublesome situations. Determine in advance how you will answer questions like "Is he yours or did you adopt him?" ("He's mine and I've adopted him.") Talk with other lesbian and gay parents (or parent groups) for advice on handling some of the trickier but basic questions of gay parenting.

The Language of Adoption

As in every situation, language conveys values. It's important to the larger world as well as to your child that you choose carefully the language you use. First and foremost, you are the child's father or parent (not "adoptive parent"). Others should refer to you as the father, too. When discussing how you became a father, use "father by adoption" (rather than "adoptive father"), since the latter term may imply that your role as a father is somehow different. Finally, the child was born to "birth parents" or "biological parents" not "natural" or "real" parents.

FOUR

HOME LIFE

*The ornament of a house is the friends who
frequent it.*

—Ralph Waldo Emerson

*E*tiquette, like charity, begins at home. What does that mean? Simple. In your home, do your best to make guests comfortable. For many, it's impossible to forget an amazing White House dinner during the Kennedy administration. A visiting monarch (whose name has been purged by the storytellers) mistook a bowl of consommé for a finger bowl. First he dipped one hand into the steamy liquid, then the other. The first lady, seated next to him, saw the king's error and quickly followed suit, dipping her young hands into the teeming soup. In the end, the entire table had washed its hands *à table,* and the king, it is said, was none the wiser. Closer to home, if Joseph breaks one of your best crystal goblets, clean up the broken shards (with a smile), mop up the wine (with a smile), and give him a new glass (and hope for the best).

This chapter covers all domestic bases, from the four fundamental elements of successful entertaining to dealing with problem guests (the crasher, the no-show, and he-who-will-not-leave), and the epidemic problem of guests with special diets. The detailed rules for overnight guests are outlined (so you can be sure to snag more weekends on the Cape or in the Napa Valley), followed by an examination of rules for seasonal households (aka having a Fire Island share), and a crash course on letter writing, including how to address envelopes to a gay couple, the lost art of the love letter, and crafting letters of condolence.

ENTERTAINING

The Rules of Entertaining

Marcel explains that when he lived with his lover they always threw a big holiday dinner in mid-December. With a full-sized kitchen, another set of helping hands, and a comfortable house, he recalls, "It was almost a piece of cake." After they broke up, Marcel moved into a cozy West Village studio with a tiny kitchen. "I was determined to have Christmas dinner for twenty that first year, no matter what," he laughs now. "This took a lot of planning: deciding on a menu, organizing the kitchen, and cooking all day. Obviously, my guests couldn't all sit around the same table, so some sat on chairs, others on pillows, and still others on the windowsill. Without my ex, it took a lot of work, but I enlisted various friends to help out. In the end, the evening was considered an unqualified success."

Where there's a will, there's a way. Certainly anybody who wants to entertain is capable. Still, how you entertain should fit into your overall lifestyle: your budget,

THE ESSENTIAL BOOK OF *Gay* MANNERS and ETIQUETTE

the size of your apartment or house, the kind of parties your circle enjoys. Entertaining need not be a formal dinner for twelve; it refers to everything from brunch for two to a small cocktail hour, to a surprise party for your lover. The reward in entertaining is providing a good time for your friends, nourishing them with delicious food and enjoyable company.

Here are the basic requisites for successful entertaining:

- Guests who have a positive (or charmingly negative) attitude and who make an effort at contributing to the group
- Good food
- A welcoming home
- A charming host!

Host Rule: Take the time to invite compatible guests, plan a menu, clean the house, shop, cook, and set up— whether it's dinner for a new boyfriend or for your lover's family. No halfway measures.

Host Rule: Make a budget and stick to it. Don't spend your monthly food budget on one night's festivities.

Host Rule: Plan so that you can enjoy the evening along with your guests. Too many hosts "work" their parties and never enjoy their guests.

Guest Rule: If someone has extended you an invitation, reciprocate within a reasonable period. Reciprocation does not mean mirroring the original event. An expensive evening of dinner and the theater can be appropriately reciprocated by a delicious home-cooked meal. It's the thought—not the expense—that counts.

> **"[To be in society is] a bore. But to be out of it simply a tragedy."**
>
> —OSCAR WILDE

The Guest List

Some say that designing a first-rate guest list requires the talents of a diplomat, psychologist, chemist, magician, and prophet. Not really. All it takes is thought and consideration—and a good pool of friends and colleagues. Even if you're a great cook, people usually leave the party talking about that "brilliant writer," that "witty scientist," and that "handsome stockbroker."

Select your guests with great care. There's no reason to invite too many clever, boisterous gents to a small dinner (each fellow needs as many listeners—not rivals—as he can get). Similarly, too many shy or quiet guests can quickly extinguish any attempt at spirited conversation. At dinner parties these days, most people allow their guests to sit wherever they please. Sometimes this

THE ESSENTIAL BOOK OF *Gay* MANNERS and ETIQUETTE

122

is fine; at other times, you may want to designate seating to facilitate specific people's getting to know each other.

Host Rule: If there's a guest of honor, he should be to your right. Sandwich quieter types in between more vocal ones; men whom you are setting up (matchmaking) should be seated across from each other.

Host Rule: If you invite one single man, invite at least another. It's difficult to be the only uncoupled fellow in a crowd.

Host Rule: When women are present, forget about seating guests boy-girl-boy-girl. Match people by their interests.

Setting the Table

Stuart was a little crazy in the kitchen, so he asked Chris to set the table for him. "No problem," said his guest, who proceeded to count out the requisite number of spoons, forks, knives, plates, salad plates, wineglasses, and water glasses. And then he froze. "I can never remember what goes where," he recalled later, almost in a panic. "I'm sure everyone in the world knows this but me. I was really embarrassed when I had to ask Stuart for a first-grade lesson in table settings."

Let's be real. Does this really matter? In the grand scheme of things, no. Even etiquette mavens like Letitia Baldrige have messed up. She recalls a fabulous black-tie dinner where she used her spoon to eat the stuffed avocado appetizer instead of the tiny fork on the far left, which was the correct implement. Many courses later, a creamy dessert was served, and poor Tish, she had only her little fork to eat it with. "To make matters worse," she wrote later of the evening, "everyone at my table had followed my lead, thinking I knew what I was doing. I had to SOS the waiter to bring spoons for our entire table."

What follows is generally considered the "right way" to set your table. However, knowing the right way doesn't mean you can't do it other ways.

DISHES: For the most formal dinner party, the place setting begins with a service plate of fine china (also known as a charger). These plates are generally twelve inches in diameter and act as a base plate for all courses. Each new course is served on a different plate. Place the bread plate to the left (actually west) of the dinner plate so that it is close to the tines of the fork farthest to the left. Place the salad plate diagonally to the upper left (northwest) of the dinner plate. A salad plate may also be placed on the service plate when it is time for that course.

CUTLERY: Cutlery is used from "the outside in." Place forks to the left of the dinner plate in order of usage (in other words, the fork farthest from the plate is used first). The same holds true for knives. Place one knife for each course (when needed) to the right of the dinner plate (blades facing "in"); again, the one used first (for an appetizer that needs cutting) is placed farthest from the plate. If serving soup as a first course, place the spoon at the extreme right (of any and all knives). The small butter knife is placed on the bread plate's upper left rim. Don't put coffee spoons on the table until coffee cups and saucers are added at the end of the meal. The dessert fork and spoon are placed directly above the dinner plate and arranged horizontally (the fork points right and the spoon left).

GLASSES: Set water glasses just above the knife at the right and wineglasses just to the left of them. If you plan to serve champagne, place the flute in place of or to the left of the wineglass.

NAPKINS: Set napkins either to the left of the fork(s) (not underneath) or on the service plate. They can also be placed in the wine or water glass, folded imaginatively. All napkins should be folded in a uniform manner—neat, pressed smooth, and easy to unfold.

Before serving dessert, clear all dishes from the table, including salt and pepper mills, wineglasses, and condiment dishes.

Guest Rule: If unsure of which utensil to use, eat from the outside in. In other words, use the fork farthest to the left (and the knife farthest to the right if you need it) for the first course. Keep moving in until all utensils are used. If all goes according to plan, there will be no more courses to come. When in doubt, follow your host's lead.

Host Rule: If you have a limited selection of cutlery, improvise. Salad forks are fine for fish, dessert, and, of course, salad. A teaspoon will do for dessert. Steak knives may also be used as fruit knives. The point in using different utensils is not to show off your silver service, but to provide a clean implement that does not carry the taste of one course to the next.

Host Rule: Set a different wineglass for each new wine to be served throughout the meal. Don't put down the dessert wineglass until the dessert is served.

"[*A cocktail party is*] an affair where you meet old friends you never met before."

—FULTON BRYAN

Smashing Cocktail Parties

How about a seriously chilled martini, dry, neat, two olives? Or a single-malt scotch on the rocks, with a soda back? Or a tall glass of sparkling water, over ice, with a twist? Everyone loves a cocktail party—as much for the opportunity to see old friends and meet new people as for the libations. A staple of gay life, these informal get-togethers are (by the way) the perfect way to set up your favorite single guys.

Despite the fact that "it's always drink time somewhere

in the world," cocktail parties should begin between five and seven in the evening, ending in time for guests to have dinner elsewhere. You may serve a full bar, sparkling drinks (champagne and sparkling water), or various wines and soft drinks. Keep in mind that more and more people don't drink alcohol; provide alternatives. For bigger parties, set up a table or bar close to the area where guests congregate. Keep a supply of clean glasses and a tray for used glasses near the bar. Food should be bite-sized; provide plates for hot appetizers; and always have lots of napkins.

Rule: The best way to end your party is to close the bar or make dinner plans yourself and leave your home.

Rule: Don't ever push an alcoholic drink on someone. Be careful about guests who become drunk. Make sure they have a safe way to get home (you may be legally responsible).

REGARDING GUESTS

Know Your Guests

Trevor and Andrew invited four friends over for drinks and dinner at their house. While Trevor greeted their guests, Andrew finished making the tarte tatin. Sam and his new boyfriend, Brett, were the first to arrive, and after a tour of the house they settled in the living room for a drink.

"What can I get you, Sam?" Trevor boomed.

"I'll have a club soda, thanks," Sam replied.

"A club soda? Wouldn't you like something to warm you up?" Trevor insisted.

"No, a club soda would be great."

After a few minutes, Andrew emerged from the kitchen. Trevor started to introduce Andrew to Sam's new boyfriend. "Andrew, I'd like you to meet Rhett."

"It's Brett," Sam interjected.

"Oh, I'm sorry," Trevor replied.

"Yes, of course. It's a pleasure to meet you," Andrew said. After ten minutes, Andrew said: "Why don't we move into the dining room?"

Once everyone was seated around the table, Trevor began to pour the wine. "No, thank you," Sam said as Trevor leaned to pour for him.

"This Beaujolais is just in. Have some. I think you'll like it," Trevor continued.

"I don't think so. You see, I'm a recovering alcoholic."

"I'm sorry, Sam," Trevor said, removing his glass. . . .

When you invite people to your home, take the trouble to know a little about each of them, so that you can make introductions and facilitate conversations. ("Oh, Brad, you know about wireless communication. This is Guy, he's a techie, too.") If a friend has a new boyfriend, ask your friend for some basic information before they arrive.

> ## "Good manners are made up of petty sacrifices."
>
> —RALPH WALDO EMERSON

Special Diets

Without question, it is difficult to know the various diet limitations and requirements people have these days. Trying to accommodate people who may be vegetarian, allergic to wheat, and repulsed by chicken on the bone can make life intolerable for a host. On the other hand, you want to serve a meal that is appreciated (and eaten) by your guests.

Host Rule: A good host attempts to determine his guests' dietary limitations and accommodates them, if possible. Since many people don't eat red meat these days, it's wiser to serve chicken or a fancy pasta dish. But hosts cannot—and should not—attempt to accommodate everyone. Simply asking "What don't you eat?" when you initially extend the invitation usually takes care of this.

Host Rule: Be respectful of your guests' medical problems, allergies, or addictions. Try to know about them in advance.

Guest Rule: Politely decline a serving of a dish you don't
want to eat. No questions should be asked. If you
have special diet restrictions, keep to them as best
you can, but don't make pronouncements at the
table.

If you have a medical problem that prohibits you
from eating certain foods (particularly food aller-
gies), by all means discuss this with your host before-
hand. The same holds true for those recovering alco-
holics who do not eat food prepared with alcohol—
even when it is cooked off.

Guest Rule: If given too large a serving or something not
to your liking, eat what you can. Move things
around on your plate to camouflage what you leave
behind.

"Civility costs nothing and buys everything."

—LADY MARY WORTLEY MONTAGU

Problem Guests

While your guests are the raison d'être of your entertaining, they also may be the bane. It's hard to know
exactly what to expect—except that you're probably
wise to expect some deviation from the plan. Whenever
possible, don't let rude guests undermine your outward
demeanor or the spirit of the party.

THE NO-SHOW: Once you've accepted an invitation, show up. It's really that simple. Many people think that saying "yes" is "maybe" and give no consideration to a host's planning. While there are legitimate excuses, a no-show guest should apologize profusely to his host as soon as is possible. Follow up with a note and/or send a bouquet of flowers. If you're a host who has heard not a peep from an absent guest, call, determine if there were any extenuating circumstances ("I was in the emergency room!"), and then be frank about the turn of events.

Guest Rule: If a crisis occurs, call your host—even if it's at the very last minute or after the event has started. He will appreciate knowing what's happening.

THE LATE GUEST: The only way to deal with people who are late is to go on without them after a reasonable—but short—period of time. If the occasion is dinner, wait at most fifteen minutes. You certainly don't want to spoil the meal for the rest of your company.

Host Rule: Don't let a late guest ruin your plan for the party. You don't want to appear inconsiderate of your other—on-time—guests.

THE CRASHER: Aside from being polite to this "guest," you certainly have no obligation to feed or entertain him. If he has simply dropped by and it's time for dinner, say, "It was great of you to stop by, but you'll have to excuse us. Our dinner is ready. Please call soon so we can make some plans." At larger parties, it is more difficult to enforce an ejection; of course, the intrusion is presumably less offensive as well.

Guest Rule: It's bad enough to ask to bring another guest; it's nearly unforgivable to simply appear.

"Never mistake endurance for hospitality."

—UNKNOWN

HE-WHO-WILL-NOT-LEAVE: In the old days, they called them "sitters." This is the guest who keeps asking for another nightcap or another cup of coffee long after your other guests have bid you goodnight. Handling this situation tactfully is a challenge, because you have invited him into your home. If your guest is drinking, don't join him. Perhaps he will notice and drink up fast. Then move on to some basic gestures, like cleaning up, yawning, or making remarks about how the evening has flown by. If none of that works, say, "Fred, it's awfully late, and since we have an early day tomorrow, we should call it a night. It was great that we got to visit as long as we did." Or pull a close friend aside and say, "I'm exhausted. Would you mind mentioning to everybody how late it is?" He then says something like "We should probably let poor Dean get some shut-eye. It's gotten awfully late." This takes the burden off you.

Guest Rule: Pay attention to the time. A rule of thumb:
Leave the party a half hour after coffee was first
served. Have consideration for your hosts; after all,
once you've gone home, they still have to clean up.

THE SMOKER: Smoking has become such a heated issue that it's hard to know the right thing to do. What is your obligation to your guests if there are smokers? What about to the nonsmokers? Many hosts feel comfortable proclaiming, "This is a nonsmoking apartment," and leave it at that. Others designate areas where smokers can puff freely. "You can smoke on the patio or in the kitchen." Whatever the case, let smokers know the situation from the start. If you put out ashtrays, expect that smokers will light up.

Rule: Do not take your party as an opportunity to lecture
smoking guests about their bad and unhealthful
habit. However, secondary smoke is dangerous and
other guests should not be made uncomfortable or
placed at risk.

Dealing With Exes

Our hosts were all excited about throwing their annual "white party"—their regular ode to spring. They had but one problem. Six months before, their good friends Hank and George "divorced" acrimoniously. In fact, the two former lovers haven't spoken to each other since then. Although the hosts had seen each of them separately, this was the first occasion where both exes were invited. "We really didn't know how to go about this. Invite both? Invite one, and the other the next time?"

This is a difficult problem for hosts and guests alike. Since you want friends to be comfortable in your home, you need to create that environment for them. In this case, it makes sense to invite both Hank and George and tell each that the other is invited (or has accepted). It is then for each ex to decide whether he wants to face the other.

Rule: No surprises—particularly when it comes to exes.
Be up front. Everyone will be more comfortable.

Rules for Houseguests

Alex climbs the six flights of stairs to his sweltering apartment, drops his briefcase, mail, and groceries on the floor before collapsing on his sofa. He peels off his sweat-soaked shirt, turns on the air conditioner, only to remember it needs a new fuse. He heads to the kitchen for a cold drink, with the refrigerator providing a welcome blast of cool air. He pulls up a chair in front of the fridge door. "Ah . . ." he declares. Suddenly, the phone rings.

"It's Simon, how are you, Alex?"

"I'm dying of heat exhaustion like everyone else in the city, but other than that just fine," he says.

"Ned and I were hoping you could join us out at the beach over the holiday weekend. We're opening the house and would love to have you come out."

"That would be great. I had such a wonderful time

last year, both with you guys and with your friends. What may I bring?"

Every gay man needs friends with a vacation house—for those winter weekends in Vermont or the long, lazy days of summer in the Hamptons. When you receive an invitation, respond promptly—certainly within the week. Find out what time you are expected to arrive, what you may bring, and whether you can help transport any other guests. (However, you can't ask, "Who else is invited?" to help you decide whether or not to accept.)

Rule: If the weather is poor or looks iffy, do not cancel. It will appear as though you value the outdoor activities more than the company of your host.

Rule: If single, do not ask to bring along another guest. If a dog or cat owner, leave Fido and Kitty with friends, at a kennel, or at home.

Rule: If you go out to a club or to the bars, do not bring a "trick" back with you—unless you know it's okay.

Rule: Bring a positive attitude. Contribute to the weekend in the best ways you can. If things aren't to your liking, don't complain. A weekend is not that long.

Rule: Bring a small but suitable houseguest present (i.e., something you know your hosts will enjoy). For instance, offer to take charge of a meal; bring a good bottle of wine or some gourmet delectables

*(just for your host); bring along a camera and take
pictures, which you can then send to your hosts as a
remembrance of the weekend. Consideration—not
dollars—is what counts.*

*Rule: After the weekend, no matter how well you know
your host, send a thank-you note.*

"No one can be so welcome a guest that he will not annoy his host after three days."

—PLAUTUS

SUMMER SHARES

Rules for Seasonal Households

"I've been going out to Fire Island every summer for
almost ten years now," says Chris. "Some summers I've
really enjoyed my housemates; other summers it's been a
complete drag. For the most part, this has nothing to do
with whether the guys are nice or not; it's all those
lifestyle things that can just drive a guy crazy. In the
eighties I used to do coke and none of my housemates
did. Now I'm in AA and the rest of my house drink. This
year people's food habits drove us over the edge: Walter
didn't eat red meat; Byron couldn't stand fish; Bob was

allergic to anything with mustard; Chuck liked to eat at 10 P.M.; I was hungry by 6 P.M. I was amazed we ever got to the table."

This is what's called "the problem of great expectations." A bunch of city guys decide to team up for the summer; there's a quick discussion about finances ("half now, half on signing"); a roughing-out of who comes which weekends; perhaps a word or two about "process"; and that's it . . . playtime.

Rule: Before you decide on a household, ask prospective members relevant lifestyle questions:

- *Do they plan to settle into "Pines time," which is to say, up by noon, tea dance at 6 P.M., a household dinner at 9 or 10 P.M., with dancing until dawn?*

- *What are the house's expectations regarding drug use, alcohol, and smoking?*

- *Are there any special diets that will cause difficulty for others?*

- *Are there any house rules on other overnight guests—either old friends or new sex partners?*

Rule: Be honest about your expectations. If a group of potential housemates doesn't seem right for you, keep looking. There are lots of great houses. (FYI: Great people are more important.)

Rule: Once you've formed a new household unit, get together and discuss the details (before the season starts): who gets which weekends, which bedrooms; will dinners be communal or catch-as-catch-can; how will expenses be divided; who will be in charge of devising a cleaning schedule; how will household problems be resolved?

Rule: Good housemates do the following: communicate well and speak frankly; respect each other; shoulder their responsibilities; clean up after themselves; take accurate phone messages; abide by any other house rules.

Dividing Expenses

There are several ways to approach the money question. Some households agree to share and divide all costs equally (from food and alcohol to the electric and phone bills). Others buy staples and specific meals together, leaving the rest of the shopping to each individual, settling accounts either on a weekly, biweekly, or monthly basis. Still other households share only the roof, with each fellow or couple doing his or their own food shopping.

Rule: Make sure all housemates are in agreement about how bills will be paid (and when). Either set up a pool from which all housemates can take money to buy household items or keep detailed records of expenses so that they can be tallied and appropriately divided. Be reasonable and considerate.

The Annoying Housemate

Over the years, it's been hard to escape the "horror" stories that have ruined many a house-share arrangement. While there are many, the following are perennials:

THE SLOB: He treats the entire house as if it's his alone, leaving wet and dirty clothing everywhere. Although he makes a pass at doing his chores, his level of cleanliness is so low it makes no difference. Generally, the slob is unaware that he's a slob.

Rule: Make a chart listing each housemate on one axis and the cleaning chores to be performed on the other. Determine who is responsible for which chores and when they are to be done.

THE NYMPH: This type has no problem picking up a guy at the beach and bringing him home for sex—either in the pool, the living room, or the bedroom the nymph shares. He cares not about the hour, the presence of others, or the decibel level.

Rule: Establish rules and live by them. Some houses don't allow for sex between housemates. Some houses simply forbid tricking. Some ask that you do your tricking elsewhere—his place, the dunes, back in the city (or that you wait until August, when, if things don't work out, summer's almost over). Still other households put condoms on the communal shopping list.

THE CONTROL FREAK: You know the type—he's up at dawn, organizing, cleaning, fretting, finishing your sentences, and, in general, insisting his way is best no matter what.

Rule: Remind him that it's summer and that island life is different from city life. Remind him that people have different ways of living. Be firm (if not a little controlling, yourself).

THE DRUNK: He starts the day with a Bloody Mary and ends it with a whiskey sour and is especially annoying when he drinks your liquor and then passes out in the living room.

Rule: Distinguish between social drinking and drunkenness. All housemates need to respect each other's values—particularly when it comes to alcohol and drugs. If you're in Alcoholics Anonymous or Narcotics Anonymous, find a non-substance-using household.

Rule: All brands are not equal. Replace what you finish.

The Privacy Problem

Part of the fun of the summer share is getting to spend "down time" with people you enjoy. Such spontaneity—whether over morning coffee, afternoon tea, or a midnight cognac—is precisely what you had in mind. Sometimes, however, you run into trouble. There's the leech—who becomes attached to your hip, whether at the beach, a party, or when you want to snuggle up and read the latest murder mystery. Of course, for those sharing bedrooms with virtual strangers, privacy can be hard to come by here, too.

Rule: You must accept some lessening of your privacy requirements if you join a communal household. If the idea of a roommate's snoring, reading after you've turned in, or basically claiming a place on this planet is too much, don't set yourself up.

Rule: Establish certain boundaries. If you want to be alone, suggest making the bedroom exclusively yours from, say, 4 to 5 P.M., and his from 5 to 6 P.M. Then you can nap, read, have sex . . . without threat of interruption. Discuss having a house "quiet hour" if that is of interest.

Sharing a Bathroom

"How much mirror time is too much?" Oskar asks. Without falling prey to gay stereotypes, there are a good number of us who—even while at the beach or in the mountains—find it necessary to spend huge quantities of time preparing for the day ahead. After all, a morning routine often includes the ritual shower, body exfoliation, teeth cleaning, nail cutting, followed by shaving, face washing, toning, moisturizing, and applying sun protection. Then, of course, there's the morning hair problem. . . . Says Oskar: "It's really only a problem if someone takes longer than me."

*Rule: If sharing bathrooms, set a time limit or make a
    schedule. Be prepared to allow for flexibility in this
    schedule. Nature knows not manners.*

The Semiresident Guest

"Seven was enough," Dom recalls of his Cherry Grove
house. "About two weeks into the season Roger began
seeing Dale, which everyone thought was great because
Roger was the only single guy among us. But pretty soon
Dale started coming out every weekend. We were comfortable at seven and, obviously, the cost had been calculated based on seven. Suddenly, it seemed to everyone—except Roger and Dale—that we were subsidizing
an eighth person. Sure, once in a while would be fine,
but not every weekend."

In any household, whether it's a summer share or
your city pied-à-terre, it's important to respect your fellow housemates. An occasional overnight visitor is fine.
However, if you start seeing a fellow on a regular basis—
and he's drinking coffee, watching TV, and otherwise
becoming a regular presence in the house—it's time to
talk. It's inconsiderate and unfair to take advantage of
housemates this way.

*Rule: Guests do not pay for their lodging and meals.
    Residents are required to. Determine in which cate-
    gory the man in question belongs.*

*Rule: You do not have the right to make your boyfriend a
    member of your summer household. If he starts to*

*become a semiresident guest, work out some form of
payment or barter arrangement with your housemates. In lieu of cash, buy the weekend's food
and/or make a festive dinner. Offer to pay the utili-
ties. Avoid the situation in which your friend
becomes known as the dreaded "freeloader."*

LETTER WRITING

How to Address Envelopes to a Gay Couple

Thank-you notes. Party invitations. Letters of condolence. As more and more couples live "out" lives, it's
become increasingly important to know how to address
invitations and correspondence to them. The following
rules are meant to reflect the realities of most relationships. In some cases, such as a committed couple who
live apart, modification of the rules is encouraged.

*Rule: Traditional etiquette stipulates separate invitations
to members of a couple who don't live together. This
rule applies even if you are better friends with one
member of the couple. If you don't know the new
boyfriend's name, ask. Just because it is easier (and
cheaper) to send one invitation doesn't make it
right. The rationale? Until a commitment is
made—either by virtue of a ceremony, living
together, or a pronouncement of love—members of
couples are treated as sovereign beings.*

*Rule: Couples who live together should be addressed
    alphabetically, on separate lines.*

MR. JOHN ARTEMIS
MR. JAMES KENNEDY
1025 Trinity Street
Durham, NC 27703

Note: This is the form to be used for unmarried but cohabiting heterosexuals. Married straight couples are typically awarded an "and" between their names to signify their union. If you understand the gay couple to have a committed relationship, use the "and" between each name and place on one line (when possible).

*Rule: Do not use the title "Messrs." when writing to a gay
    couple. It is used as a title for two or more brothers.*

*Rule: If one member of a couple has a higher rank, his
    name comes first:*
JUDGE TOM FRANKEL AND MR. PETER STEIN

Rule: When both are doctors (or judges), list alphabetically:
DR. WILLIAM REINHARDT AND DR. LOUIS ZOLA

The Lost Art of the Love Letter

With answering machines, e-mail, personal digital assistants, and a host of other electronic devices, few, if any of us, actually take pen to paper to write to the one we love. What a pity! When's the last time you wrote some sweet nothing to your man or vice versa?

Gordon still has the piles of tattered, yellowed sheets from his ex-lover Ellis tied up with a thick string. One of his favorites ends with a poem by Cavafy:

> And there on the much-used, lowly bed
> I had the body of love, I had the lips,
> the voluptuous and rosy lips of ecstasy—
> rosy lips of such ecstasy, that even now
> as I write, after so many years!
> in my solitary house, I am drunk again.

Rule: If you are in love with a man, let him know it by putting it down on paper. Tell him and write him often. You can quote poetry, list his wonderful qualities, or just say, "I love you." Caveat: Don't let passion cause you to make promises you can't keep.

Rule: If you are coupled with someone else, think twice, even three times, before you commit yourself on paper to another man. This could backfire on you.

> ## *"When angry, count four; when very angry, swear."*
>
> —MARK TWAIN

A Caution about Penning Angry Thoughts

Broken hearts, take heed:

Luke—

I'm enclosing various things found around the apartment that reek of you. The stench of your unfulfilled intimacy may now be lessened. You wasted over two years of my life—a major burden to me and most of my friends. You are disgusting, not only in how you have shamelessly treated me, but in your inability to see beyond your problems. I wish you the worst life has to offer. It may then come close to how you have treated me. You really blew happiness. You really did.

—Hugo

This is the perfect example of a letter that should have been written, reread several times aloud in front of a mirror to good effect, and then torn up and rewritten to express more moderate and less embarrassing sentiments. We all get angry—even furious—particularly when it comes to matters of the heart. But in most cases this anger dissipates into cooler, more rational feelings.

In writing this kind of letter, it's important to stay focused on the purpose: to convey exactly why you are angry. If that message gets lost in overheated and under-reasoned rhetoric, what good have you done yourself? Moreover, the last thing you want —months or years later—is for someone to have evidence of you at your absolute worst.

Rule: If you feel so angry that you must get it off your chest, write a letter. Put it aside for three days—or at least overnight. Then reread it and decide whether it's appropriate to send. If not, throw it away. If in doubt, ask a close friend to look at it.

Rule: When you sit down to write, outline your complaints and write in a controlled—unemotional— voice. Generally, sarcasm won't advance your case.

Rule: Remember, some things are actually better said in the heat of passion than written. At least that way there's no evidence to be held against you.

Notes of Apology

The importance of the apology in smoothing social relations cannot be overstated. For those circumstances in which a verbal "I'm sorry" just doesn't do the trick (situations that come to mind include ruining a dinner party by being drunk and sloppy, forgetting a date, failing to fulfill a pledge to an AIDS organization), it's a good idea to pen a short letter or note of apology. These letters need not be long or involved, but they must express sincere sentiment.

Rule: Keep notes short but to the point. Be explicit about what you are apologizing for. If at all possible present a credible reason for your error. Take responsibility for your action or lack thereof. If you have broken something—and it was an act of carelessness—either offer to replace the item or, if you know where it was purchased, do so yourself.

A sample note:

Dear Ed,

I want to apologize again for spilling the red wine on your new down comforter. Mother always said not to smoke or drink in bed . . . and I see she is right again. I understand that the dry cleaner gave up on cleaning it after the fifth time. I've taken the liberty of ordering a new one for you. I hope to be invited to spend the night again sometime soon.

Love,
Buzz

Sometimes the mistake is so egregious that there is literally nothing you can do other than profess your complete and utter sorrow.

A sample note:

> Dear Bob,
>
> I know that words will never suffice for my inconsiderate action last night. I can't tell you how sorry I am that I inadvertently revealed your HIV status. I had thought you had told Charlotte about the test results, but I see now that conversation should not be based on supposition. Again, I apologize.
>
> Sincerely,
> Matthew

Thank-You Notes

After an anniversary party, José started writing thank-you notes to each guest who had brought a present. To save time, he decided to write the same note to everyone. Said José: "It seemed unlikely that anyone would compare notes." His lover, Alexander, took one look at the notes and threw them away. "José," he said. "You really need to mention their specific gifts. If they went to the trouble to get us a set of embroidered place mats, the least we can do is mention the gift by name."

Rule: All gift givers should be thanked with a note. Be as specific as you can. Be as timely as you can. After two weeks, you are derelict. After a month, you are hopelessly rude.

Rule: Thank-you notes should also be penned for all formal dinners and parties, tickets (theater, opera, bal-

*let, and sporting events), weekend events, and all
favors (a friend who takes care of your ill lover for
the day so you can take some time off, or a friend
who sets you up with a professional contact). If this
is just not your style, call to say thank you.*

"Grief would have tears, and sorrow bids me speak."

—WILLIAM SHAKESPEARE

Letters of Condolence

Nearly every etiquette book takes note of the great challenge faced in writing a letter of condolence. Death is not a topic that many of us are comfortable with. Expressing on paper our emotions about the death of a friend, colleague, or relative can be even more difficult. AIDS adds to these challenges; more often than not, we are talking about the death of a relatively young man (or woman), someone in the prime of his life, someone, truly, with much to live for.

When someone dies, you may send flowers, make a donation to a charity in his or her name, attend the memorial or funeral service, but a letter of condolence still remains to be penned.

*Rule: Write a letter of condolence to the bereaved person
with whom you had the closest relationship. If a good
friend dies and his lover survives him (also a friend of*

yours), write to the lover, not his family (although you may write to them as well). If a couple has broken up and yet remained friendly, it is appropriate to write to the surviving former spouse or lover.

Rule: *Write us soon as it is possible for you to collect your thoughts and express your sentiments. Try to write within a two-week period. At that time your emotions will be more completely present, allowing you to fully express yourself. If, however, you learn of someone's death many months after it occurred (say, through your college alumni magazine), it is never too late to write expressing your sorrow.*

Rule: *The length of your letter or note is much less important than its content and expression of sentiment. Whatever the length, three elements should be covered in each case:*

- *Start your letter or note by acknowledging the loss and how you learned of the person's death (from a friend, obituary, company e-mail). Register your upset, dismay, and loss. Even when someone has had a long illness—such as AIDS— the actual death can prove extremely wrenching to the survivors.*

- *Relate personal memories of the deceased (if you knew him or her); this helps the bereaved to more fully see how the loved one was appreciated by others. If you did not know the deceased, it's fine to relate anecdotes and incidents you have heard from others. Always be as specific as you can (recall political campaigns or marches, travels together . . .). Discuss how the deceased enriched your professional or personal life.*

- *If you mean it, offer genuine assistance. Many sympathy letters end with the cliché sentence: "If I can be of any assistance at this time, please don't hesitate to call me." This puts the burden on the bereaved to take action by calling you. It makes more sense to make a specific offer ("I'd be happy to do your grocery shopping this week," or "I'm sure you'll be busy this week; why don't I walk your dog for you at noontime?" or "I'd be pleased to help telephone friends with news of Tom's death"). In each case, mention that you will follow up by phone and then do so. Remember: It's only a cliché if you don't mean it or follow through.*

A sample note:

Dear Melinda,

Vladimir called me last night to say that Preston died. Even though he had been ill for some time, I find it hard to think of our lives going forward without him. I can only imagine what your loss must encompass. I'll be at the memorial next month, but will also call soon to see how I can help you.

XOXO, Steven

A sample letter when you didn't know the person who died:

Dear Martin:

This morning at staff meeting we were told the sad news that Robert had died. Although I never had the pleasure of meeting Robert, I want you to know how sorry I am and to acknowledge that this must be a very difficult time for you. I still remember when the two of you returned from the Southwest last year . . . what a trip you described . . . and how much fun you both had. From everything you ever said, Robert sounds like he was a very special man. While we've had mostly a business relationship, I've watched you persevere through many difficult situations. During this tough time, I'm sure you'll draw on those same resources so many of us admire to carry you through.

While you are out, I'll take the responsibility for covering your accounts. Bear in mind that there are many in the office who send their deepest sympathy.

Sincerely,
Ronald

Sympathy Cards

Old-world etiquette strictly prohibited the use of store-bought sympathy cards. The prevailing thought was that death was a time for the true expression of the heart, which cannot be captured in a mass-produced card. While we agree in principle, there are many people who are deterred by facing the blank page of a letter of condolence and who, in the end, write or send nothing to the bereaved. It's better to send a card you buy than none at all.

Rule: If you send a store-bought sympathy card, pen a short note at the bottom. Similarly, if you are sending preprinted thank-you cards, a short note adds much to your response.

What Not to Write

Longfellow said it best: "There is no grief like the grief which does not speak." Very few people know what to write to the survivors of a friend or family members. Many of us fear writing a letter of condolence because we may say the wrong thing. Keep it simple and genuine: explain how sorry you are to hear the news, how much you liked or loved the deceased, and how you will miss him. One thing is certain: grace of expression or eloquence plays second if not third fiddle to sincerity. Do not spend endless hours toying with your wording. Be honest in expressing your loss. On the other hand, certain phrases should be avoided. These include:

- Try to get on with your life.
- Don't cry.
- I know exactly what you're going through.
- His death was really a blessing. You must be relieved.
- You were lucky to be with him for so long.
- Don't take it so hard.
- I heard you're not taking it very well.
- You'll be out dating in no time at all.

FIVE

FASHION AND THE MAN

I hold that gentleman to be the best dressed whose dress no one observes.

—ANTHONY TROLLOPE

Cary Grant. William Holden. Clark Gable. David Niven. There's something about a man with style. He looks smart, in control, and confident about both his personality and physical appearance. Every man wants to be perceived that way, but many don't know how to accomplish it. Most fashion experts advocate one of two ideals: classic preppydom, say J. Crew and Brooks Brothers, or Milanese fashion à la Versace or Armani. Why should all gay men subscribe to the same look or couple of looks? Our credo: Individuality combined with smart information will help you develop a good personal style (but don't forget the importance of well-made and well-tailored clothes and the perfect haircut to make you shine). Above all, looking great has little to do with spending a lot of money.

While the whole world seems to be getting increasingly casual ("casual dress Fridays"), that isn't an excuse for a sloppy appearance. Nowadays, specialty stores abound on practically every street corner, offering terrific "weekend wear" and athletic clothing that carry you almost anywhere. But don't let the stores offering mass-produced clothing constitute your entire shopping horizon. Visit local boutiques and secondhand stores where you'll find an entire world of well-made, unique, and affordable clothing and accessories. With the proper guidance, you can develop a great wardrobe that is neither fussy nor lackluster.

PROPER DRESS

The Importance of Good Fit and Proper Care

To some, it's tragic to see a man who has spent a lot of time and money on clothes that don't fit him properly or show that he doesn't know how to care for them. Donald Charles Richardson, a noted fashion writer, has described the well-dressed man as someone "who appears as if he's owned his clothes for a long time, tossed them on without thought, and wears them without regard. But he can do this only if he has chosen his clothes carefully, had them meticulously fitted, and maintains them perfectly." For most men, it's actually quite possible to buy off the rack suits, jackets, and trousers that fit well. But if tailoring is called for, spend the small sum to make it just right. Clothes that fit properly will not only make you look better but are likely to make you feel more comfortable, too.

Rule: Go for simple styles and cuts, combined with basic colors (black, brown, charcoal, navy, and khaki). Choose easy-to-care-for fabrics that don't compro-

mise either looks or comfort. Choose styles, cuts, and colors that make an easy transition from year to year.

Rule: When you are choosing clothing and accessories, keep in mind that a good wardrobe should build year after year. Extremes in fashion quickly become dated.

Rule: Never wear clothing that is too tight. If it looks as though it's being stretched, it is. If you have outgrown the garment, wait until you've dropped a few pounds before you wear it again (even if it's your favorite shirt). Be careful about clothing that is too large. People who wear blowsy or oversized clothes often look sloppy, if not heavier.

Rule: Don't wear pants that are either not long enough or too long. A man's height doesn't fluctuate; neither should his inseam. Dress pants should break just above the heel, and casual slacks and jeans slightly higher.

Rule: If you have wide shoulders, avoid shoulder pads, which will make you look unnecessarily bulky (something like an overstuffed linebacker).

Rule: If a garment indicates "dry clean only" that's how you should care for it. Care labels are designed to make your life easier and to extend the life of the garment. Read them. Obey them.

SUITS AND SPORT COATS: Every man should work up to having at least four suits: a gray flannel suit, a navy wool pinstripe or solid double-breasted suit, a single-breasted black wool crepe suit, and a solid-color lightweight cotton or cotton-blend suit. To be perfectly appointed, you'll also need a navy tropical wool blazer, a tweed sport coat, and a solid-color lightweight cotton or cotton-blend sport coat.

Before purchasing a suit:

- Tug on the seams of the jacket, the trousers, and the vest to make sure they are well-stitched. Hanging threads are always a sign of poor workmanship.
- Inspect the suit's lining. Be sure it is firmly attached, or it will hang out after a few trips to the dry cleaner.
- Crumple the fabric with your hand and see if it bounces back into shape. If it creases easily or looks sloppy, that's an indication of low quality.
- Avoid unusual colors and odd-size lapels. Suits should not be trendy.

"My clothes keep my various selves buttoned up together, and enable all these otherwise irreconcilable aggregates of psychological phenomena to pass themselves off as one person."

—LOGAN PEARSALL SMITH

DRESS SHIRTS: We've all heard how some men will give you the shirts off their backs. Well, if it's the right shirt, even the most generous man might hesitate. Before you buy any shirt, have someone qualified take your collar and sleeve measurements and then write them down. Once you have this information, you're ready to make the right purchase. Buy only shirts that are your size (you wouldn't buy shoes a size smaller or larger than your own, would you?). Avoid shirts that are sized in multiple sleeve lengths, such as—31/32, 33/34, and so on, that is, unless your arms tend to lengthen and shrink from day to day.

Quality is the first thing to look for when you pick up a shirt. Your best bet is single-needle tailoring; this means that high-stress seams are sewn in twin rows, one at a time. Poor-quality shirts have seams that are sewn simultaneously, and they are apt to pucker. Pleats where the sleeve attaches to the cuff are also indications of good tailoring. A cheap shirt has gathered or tapered sleeves that don't allow for the looseness in the arm necessary for a good fit. Be sure that the pattern lines match up, that buttons are securely attached, and pockets are sewn on straight. Cotton is easy to care for. Crepe de chine looks great, but it's just impossible to care for. Linen is nice without a tie (top button closed), but wrinkles if you look at it. They're also doing some great things lately with microfiber (formerly the dreaded polyester).

Rule: Choose shirts with a minimum of seven buttons down the front; the more buttons you have, the better secured the shirt will be in your trousers.

Rule: Don't allow your cuff links or buttons to show when your arms are at your side.

Rule: Monogramming is a personal choice, but why do you need your initials on your pocket or sleeve?

Rule: Buy a variety of long-sleeved Oxford-cloth and other cotton dress shirts in solid white, pinstripes, and light blue.

Rule: If you're overweight, avoid shirts with horizontal stripes; this style will only make your midsection appear larger.

CASUAL SHIRTS: Every well-dressed man needs a few of the following shirts. Long-sleeved: cotton denim, flannel, chambray, and a selection of mock-turtle and turtleneck shirts in solid colors. Short-sleeved: cotton madras, white and black T-shirts, and solid-color polo shirts.

TROUSERS: Choose colors that are restrained and easily interchangeable: gray flannels; olive, stone, or taupe chinos; and lightweight wool-blend pants in medium brown and navy.

Rule: When buying trousers, try to choose those with an extra button behind the fly. That button supports the waistband, giving you added security.

TIES: Your tie is probably the first clothing element people notice when meeting you, so it should be one of your most considered wardrobe items. Buy silk ties (or the occasional wool or linen one), since polyester ties tend to wrinkle easily, ravel, and don't wear very well. Patterns, colors, and designs are purely personal, but coordinate ties with the texture and color of your suit.

Rule: Tall men need extra-long ties. Stocky men can often benefit from a wider tie.

How to Tie Your Tie: Believe it or not, the way you tie your tie can help you choose a shirt. If you are fond of a large knot, such as a half-Windsor, choose a spread-collar shirt because it will accommodate the knot without appearing too crowded. If you love a small tight knot, choose long-point collars. Tie your tie so that the point hits just slightly below your belt buckle. Make sure it covers all of your shirt buttons, but isn't so long that it bunches up in your lap when you sit down. When selecting a tie, use this simple test to see if it's made well. Hold the tie in the middle and allow it to drape over your hand; the two ends will fall together. The narrow end of the tie should line up exactly with the V of the wider end. If it doesn't work, the stitching is most likely crooked, and the tie will not lie properly when worn.

Rule: Your knot should cover the top shirt button and lie firmly against the neck.

Rule: Learn how to tie your own bow tie and never, ever, wear a clip-on. If you have a big neck, it is best to avoid bow ties because they tend to give your face a rounder appearance.

SHOES: The basic black dress shoe of choice is a plain black cap-toe Oxford. It's a classic and a thoroughly respectable business shoe. Duplicate the same shoe in dark brown. Wing tips are all-American but tend to look clunky if paired with the wrong suit. A classic American square-cut suit is the best match for those beloved wing tips. While on the subject of shoes, don't forget that age-old "white-dress-shoe rule" prohibiting the wearing of said item other than between Memorial Day and Labor Day (the same prohibition applies also to white slacks and suits).

Rule: Black shoes are the only acceptable footware to wear with tuxedos. The leather should be smooth and spit-shined to perfection. Patent-leather dress shoes, seamless lace-ups, and low-slung couture slippers are all acceptable styles.

Rule: Shop for shoes late in the day to ensure proper fit. Your feet are smaller in the morning and tend to swell during the day. Most men's left feet and right feet are actually different sizes; always buy the larger shoe size.

SOCKS: Business attire calls for knee highs so that when you cross your legs you don't flash bare calf. Match colors and textures to what you're wearing.

Rule: Don't wear black socks with sneakers.

Rule: Don't wear white dress socks with black street shoes (especially if you're wearing shorts).

Rule: Don't wear socks with holes (you never know when you'll have to take off your shoes).

BELTS: When choosing the appropriate belt, let your shoes do the talking. Be sure that your belt matches your shoes in both color and style. Dress shoes call for an elegant and slim belt, while casual shoes allow for a wider one.

Rule: Your belt should be darker than your suit or sport coat and slacks.

Rule: Belts should have at least five holes, and the actual length of the belt should be measured from the center hole. Your belt size is two inches greater than your waist measurement.

Rule: Cowboy boots make choosing a belt fun and give you the opportunity to bend the rules. There's nothing like a great hand-tooled leather belt with an impressive sterling-silver buckle to give your jeans a lift.

Formal Attire

What to wear to a black-tie affair? In almost all cases if the invitation reads "black tie" or "formal attire," the classic black dinner suit, aka tuxedo, is called for. In the summer, you may substitute a white dinner jacket along with the traditional black trousers. However, many men choose to wear a dark business suit to formal events.

When the invitation reads "business attire suggested," wear a dark suit. When the invitation reads "informal" or "casual," call the host and ask what he'll be wearing. It's unlikely you'll be receiving very many "white tie" invitations, but if you do, here's the dress code: tailcoat of black wool and silk, white piqué tie with a stiff wing collar, starched white shirtfront, white waistcoat, black patent pumps, pearl (or diamond or onyx) cuff links and studs, white kid gloves, and (optional) a black silk top hat. Aren't you glad you know that?

TUXEDOS: While tuxedos are now available in many styles and in a choice of fabrics, stick to basic black. The trousers should have black satin stripes down the sides. The vest is optional, but discard it if you wear a cummerbund.

Rule: Your bow tie (black is preferable) should match the facing on your lapels (either satin or grosgrain) and your cummerbund.

Rule: A simple vest may be worn with a tuxedo, but it is generally reserved for white-tie occasions.

Rule: Double-breasted tuxedos require neither a cummerbund nor vest; they do require a full-front tuxedo shirt.

Rule: Under no circumstances wear a tuxedo in a color such as robin's egg blue. Your prom days are over.

FORMAL SHIRTS: Tuxedo shirts should be simple, pleated, and solid white. Although manufacturers are turning out variations, keep it simple.

Rule: If you wear a wing collar, be sure to tuck the collar points behind the bow tie.

Rule: French cuffs, tasteful cuff links, and studs are preferable with formal attire.

Rule: Don't even consider ruffles. Guy Lombardo you are not.

STUDS: The choice of studs indicates that a man pays particular attention to the finest details of dressing. (For anyone confused, studs are the three little fasteners used in lieu of buttons to keep a man's formal shirt from falling open to reveal his chest, no matter how built it is.) Although many men favor a white broadcloth shirt with buttons, proper black-tie dress calls for a formal shirt with studs.

Studs do, however, present a variety of problems. Fastening them through your starched shirt without mussing it is often vexing; if possible get your lover/ boyfriend/roommate to help. Also, some shirt makers are now making dress shirts with four holes to accommodate men who prefer to forgo a cummerbund. If you have only sets of three, add a cummerbund or an elegant vest.

Rule: *Keep your studs, collar pins, and cuff links in good order and in boxes. If you lose one, the remainder are useless.*

"Beware of all enterprises that require new clothes."

—HENRY DAVID THOREAU

A Note on Accessories

No matter how fine your manner of dress or how well-bred you are (or pretend to be), small details can detract from your overall image. Remember, less is more.

Rule: *Use jewelry sparingly, always to enhance what you are wearing. A simple ring, an attractive watch, and the occasional and tasteful gold or silver chain is all the jewelry a man should attempt at any one time (that is, unless you're a Liberace wannabe).*

Rule: *Sunglasses were created to be worn outside, so when you come in, take them off (unless you have a legitimate medical reason).*

Rule: *Buy eyeglasses that complement the shape of your face and current hairstyle. Choose a look that paral-*

lels your overall style (that way you won't find your-self buying this year's new "look" each season).

"[Fashion] wears out more apparel than the man."

—WILLIAM SHAKESPEARE

The Basics

We've compiled this list of "must have" clothing and accessories that *will* make your life easier, sexier, and more stylish:

A faded pair of blue jeans

A pair of black jeans

An elegant white shirt that you can wear without a tie, jacket, or sport coat

A good-quality leather jacket

A pair of Ray-Bans, preferably Wayfarer or Aviator style

A sweater so warm and luxurious that you could sleep in it

A smart cardigan sweater

Two black or charcoal turtlenecks of different weights

A topcoat that falls below the knee

A good wallet

An elegant watch

Two bathrobes (his and his)

Silk boxers for romantic evenings

An elegant dinner jacket (a good-condition vintage
one is a real find)

Studs and collar stays

A fog-free shaving mirror

A sewing kit that doesn't say Hilton on it

A suede brush

A lint brush

Tweezers

The name of a great dry cleaner and an impeccable
tailor

Condoms and lots of them

"The soul of this man is his clothes."

—WILLIAM SHAKESPEARE

The Fully Equipped Leatherman

Let's start with the rule!

Rule: Leathermen wear only black leather.

ARTICLE NO. 1: The "bar vest"—worn only with a white T-shirt or no shirt at all.

NO. 2: A pair of regulation boots—only motorcycle, lace-up work boots, or engineer's boots will do. Always, always black!

NO. 3: A harness—make sure it crosses in the front and back, is belted at the waist, and has a strap that runs between the legs.

NO. 4: A pair of chaps or leather pants.

NO. 5: The leather jacket—must be a motorcycle jacket, better if previously owned, i.e., used.

NO. 6: A black leather belt—known as the Garrison belt, which is 1⅞ inches wide with a prominent and hard square buckle.

NO. 7: The black leather cap—in the same style that Marlon Brando made famous in *The Wild One* (the Union soldier cap and German student cap are now also acceptable head wear).

ACCESSORIES: There are several optional items: the wrist band (aka the vanbrace), the double-strap wrist brace, fingerless officer's or driving gloves, and mirrored sunglasses.

GEAR: No leatherman would be caught without his handcuffs, dog collar, paddle, whips, flogger, restraints, or a riding crop (not carried publicly).

GOOD GROOMING

Always Look Your Best

Everyone—from colleagues and close friends to casual acquaintances—makes judgments about you based on your appearance. Although it's been said that you can't judge a book by its cover, many gay men do.

Consider Terry's dilemma: "I wear smart suits and arrive immaculately groomed to work each day, look my best when I go out at night, but dress like a slob the rest of the time. My problem is that every time I'm sloppily dressed and unshaven and venture into the daylight, I run into everyone I know. Suddenly, I'm face-to-face with the guy that I'm going out with on Friday (and, of course, he's the height of weekend fashion and style). I shrink in my rumpled cotton shorts and torn T-shirt and blurt out, 'Sorry about the way I look. I'm rebuilding a carburetor.' 'Terry,' my-date-to-be says, 'I didn't know you had a car.' 'I don't. . . .' My question is 'Do I have to look like a movie star whenever I leave the house, or is it okay to be a slob on the weekends?'"

Nobody expects real people to look like movie stars. Terry, like many, has a problem of consistency. With a standard grooming routine in place during the week, he abandons it on weekends. Our advice: Develop a more realistic grooming routine for the entire week and stick to it. It's one thing to be disheveled; it's another to be a slob. Even if you're only going to the 7-Eleven for a grape Slurpee, there's no telling who you'll meet along the way, so try to look your best.

Rule: Don't neglect your hygiene. Bad breath, body odor, and nasty hair are real turn-offs. While you needn't go full Hollywood every day (especially not on weekends), set some minimum standards. Avoid wearing wrinkled (unless it's linen), torn (unless that's your look), or soiled clothing (no exceptions) unless you actually are rebuilding a carburetor or work on a farm.

Rule: Casual clothing doesn't mean clothes that are worn-out, too small, too big, or intended to be worn as underwear. Good taste is good taste everywhere.

> ## *"Illusion is the secret of beauty."*
> —GEORGE MASTERS

Scent of a Man

Everyone knows Harry's arrived—even before he enters the room. Despite an Ivy League education, the guy's never mastered the proper application of cologne. Says a good friend (who keeps his distance): "With Harry, a splash becomes a drenching, and what was beautiful becomes overbearing. I think cologne on a man is very intoxicating, but—as in all things—moderation."

Cologne should be applied sparingly to your pulse points. A little cologne behind each ear is sexy, and the same goes for the base of the throat. Why on the pulse points? It's there that body heat surfaces most easily and is intensified by blending with your own body chemistry. *Et voilà.* A little goes a long way.

Rule: Tolerate dissenting views. Some people find all scents repugnant, believing that there is nothing better than a scent-free man.

Essential Advice on Hair Care

Hair is the only accessory that Mother Nature included in the package. It's also one of the first things that people notice about you. Paramount to good hair care is keeping it clean and healthy. Choose a cut that works well with the natural characteristics of your hair and the shape of your face, and one that requires minimal maintenance. Try to find a style that doesn't require a lot of styling products or the use of a blow dryer. Damage from styling, coloring, perming, and straightening can never be repaired, except with a pair of scissors. Restorative hair-care products fix what is wrong with your hair only temporarily—so take care of it from the start.

Rule: If someone you know has thinning hair or a "bald patch," refrain from commenting (it may be the result of the march of time or a side effect of a med-

ical treatment). If suffering from hair loss, don't go overboard in trying to cover it up.

Rule: *If you find yourself wanting an entirely new look, wait one haircut. If you still want it, then do it.*

Rule: *If you decide to color your hair, make sure only your hairdresser knows for sure. Get it done right.*

The Plastic Surgeon and You

"Are looks really that important?" two plastic surgeons were asked. According to Drs. Joseph Giunta and George Miller: "Yes and no. Most people would agree that what is inside a person is more important than what's outside. But increasingly we're learning that the outside is pretty important too, because it can have a direct impact on how you feel about yourself. When there's something you don't like about the way you look, it can make you feel self-conscious. Unconfident. And unhappy. . . . Think of plastic surgery as a little change on the outside that can lead to a big change on the inside. That's what plastic surgery is really all about. Big changes . . . on the inside."

Nearly fifty thousand men a year have one kind of cosmetic surgery or another, whether it be a facelift, an eye job, a tummy tuck, or acne-scar removal. In cities like Los Angeles and New York, it is estimated that 70 percent of the men going under the knife are gay. Before making a decision, doctors suggest you think carefully about what you expect the surgery to do for you: Correct a medical condition? Recapture your lost youth? Improve your self-esteem? Or enhance a specific feature of your appearance? Don't go because you can't get enough dates, are lonely, or expect the procedure to change your whole life.

Rule: *Make sure your surgery is done by a reputable doctor with experience in the specific surgery you desire. Don't go to someone because he's known to have "done so and so." Choose a doctor who is board-certified. Ask your friends and colleagues for recommendations.*

Rule: *Shop around before you make a final decision. Ask to see before and after photographs of the doctor's work. Find a surgeon you can talk to—and who can hear what it is you want.*

Rule: *If you're HIV-positive, it's smart to talk with your primary-care physician before undergoing any elective surgery.*

Body Piercing

No matter what part of your body you intend to have pierced, there are several important criteria to remember. Choose a professional body piercer (he or she should be certified by a reputable piercer) who is well trained in safety and hygiene procedures. A piercer should always properly clean the area to be pierced, wear a new pair of disposable latex gloves, use a new, sterile needle for each client, and sterilize all other implements in an autoclave between uses. Unless these techniques are adhered to, you could risk getting a serious infection, such as hepatitis or HIV. Never let anyone insert jewelry directly from another person to you because of the risk of infection.

Rule: Before choosing a piercer, ask how long he or she has been piercing (and how long he or she has been trained to do the specific piercing you want; an earlobe is different from a nostril). Talk to other customers and, if possible, view their piercings.

Rule: Always use noncorrosive metals (surgical stainless steel, solid 14 karat gold, or niobium) in fresh piercings. Don't use sterling silver, gold-plated, or gold-filled jewelry.

Rule: When choosing jewelry, bear in mind its ultimate purpose. Is it primarily decorative, or do you plan on using it as a sex prop? How you use it will help you determine the wire gauge of your jewelry (thinner wire is better for decorative jewelry; use thicker wires for other uses).

Rule: Always follow the after-care suggestions given to you by your piercer. Otherwise, a serious infection could develop.

The Right Answer to "How Do I Look?"

Consider this all-too-familiar scenario: Cal and Miguel are getting ready to go out to their friend's birthday party. Miguel emerges from the bathroom in tight red jeans, a gold and rust-colored shirt, and a baggy black V-neck sweater. "How do I look?" flies out of Miguel's mouth. Cal freezes. He never tells Miguel what he really thinks of his outfits, because, well, Miguel usually doesn't take it too well. "I'm not sure it works," Cal says hesitantly.

"Why, what's wrong with it?" Miguel asks defensively.

"Nothing's wrong with it per se. I just think you could choose something better."

"Better how?" Miguel persists.

"Well, your jeans don't go with the shirt and the sweater is *very* big on you," Cal replies.

"It's supposed to be oversized."

"That's fine, but with those jeans being so tight, you look, umm, top-heavy."

"Well, if that's all true, why didn't you tell me that two weeks ago when I asked you about the same outfit?" Miguel snaps back.

How many times have we had to answer this awful question? How many times have we lied? The real question here is "Do I tell my friend the truth or something to make him feel better?" Usually, the question is asked with no time to spare. Your friend is about to go to a party, leave for a date, or go on a job interview.

Rule: If you can give advice that a person can act on immediately, do so. You will save him from himself. If he can't do anything about his fashion faux pas, let it go and take him shopping soon.

Rule: If he's about to go in front of a crowd, be encouraging (this is as close as we'll get to suggesting you lie). There's no use in telling someone he looks bad just before he steps in front of two hundred people.

Rule: Never ask this question if you can't handle the answer. You're soliciting someone's advice; don't get angry at him for being honest.

Rule: Don't say things like "You'd look a lot better if you lost forty pounds or so." He's not asking you if he looks trim; he wants to know if his blazer looks good with his slacks. Stick to the question asked.

SIX

AIDS: BEYOND MANNERS

My sense of sisterhood is showing when I say that it is totally reprehensible for a man who is bisexual to have an affair with or marry a woman who thinks he is straight. He is putting her life and that of her future children in danger because of the possibility of transmitting the HIV infection to her. There are no sexual manners that can relate to this kind of deceit.

—LETITIA BALDRIGE, *LETITIA BALDRIGE'S COMPLETE GUIDE TO THE NEW MANNERS FOR THE '90S*

*I*s it a sign of progress when HIV has finally become an entry in a mainstream manners book? Not when the judgments are so severe and the information so wrong. Certainly traditional etiquette guides have spoken eloquently, and at length, on the forms and rituals concerning illness, death, and mourning. And with good reason. At no other time have so many of us wanted to know how to act, what to say, and what to do. Said Emily Post in her *Blue Book of Social Usage*: "At the time of actual bereavement, when we stand baffled and alone, etiquette performs its most real service by smoothing the necessary personal contacts and making sure that the last rites of our beloved shall be performed with beauty and gravity."

AIDS has presented the gay community (and, of course, the larger world) with an entirely new set of difficult dilemmas and painful situations. What to say when a friend tests positive. How to reveal your own status. When to ask a date about his HIV status. What to do about HIV-related rumors (concerning friends or coworkers). Doctor and hospital etiquette has also taken on new dimensions as our friends with HIV disease go to their physicians, seek experimental treatments, need hospital care, and, in all too many instances, die.

In this chapter, these questions and many others are addressed, resulting in a significant revision of traditional manners and mores. The final section of the chapter focuses on funerals and memorial services—everything from facing off with homophobic relatives of the deceased to writing a gay-specific death notice.

"This disease will be the end of many of us, but not nearly all," wrote Tony Kushner, the Pulitzer Prize–winning playwright of *Angels in America*. He then added, "You are fabulous creatures, and I bless you. More life."

THE TEST

Deciding to Take the HIV Antibody Test

Since its development in the mid-1980s, the HIV antibody test has been the subject of much controversy, not the least of which is the issue of an individual's right to privacy. Who else will find out your status: your boss, your health-insurance company, your landlord, the government? Who else do you want to tell: your friends, your family, men you date?

If you decide to take the HIV antibody test, find a test site that offers pre- *and* post-test counseling (where trained counselors explain your results and can provide additional medical or therapeutic referrals, if necessary). Your local public health department or an AIDS hot line is a good resource for this information. Because of the possibility of being discriminated against, or of losing your health insurance, go to a site where results are kept confidential, if not anonymous.

There's no longer any question that early detection of HIV is crucial. The overriding benefit is the monitoring of the infection, of T-cell counts, and of other markers of disease, so that appropriate treatments can be started when necessary. Early treatment slows the progression of disease and can delay the onset of specific illnesses, such as *Pneumocystis carinii* pneumonia. Testing can buy you time!

Rule: If you think you may be infected and have not been tested, get tested. If you have a friend in the same situation, urge him to get tested.

Rule: Anonymous testing is preferred because it guarantees complete anonymity. Anonymous testing has been shown to encourage individuals who otherwise might fear disclosure to come in and be tested. Confidential testing is second best. Other than yourself, only your doctor or health-care provider needs access to your results.

If You Test Positive

"I took the antibody test three years ago," says Stephen, a Milwaukee radio producer. "That was something. It took me two years to get up the courage to go to the public health department. I kept hearing two voices in my head, one saying, 'You should know what's going on in your body,' and the other, 'You're terrified, you'd rather just not deal with it.' Finally, reason and various public education campaigns prevailed. I had read enough by that time to know that I could be doing a really good thing for myself by getting tested. Still, I talked with my friend Philip *forever* about this and then one day we both decided to go to the local health clinic."

Philip tested negative, Stephen positive.

For Stephen, the questions quickly became: Whom to tell? When? Where? How much to explain? The decision about whom to tell of a newly diagnosed HIV infection can be difficult and wrenching. "How will my parents react?" "Will my friends abandon me?" "Will my lover dump me?" "Will my job be safe?"

Often the disclosure of your HIV status also means the simultaneous disclosure of other aspects of your life, for instance, that you're gay or have used intravenous drugs. For some, the combined weight of these disclosures can be paralyzing.

Rule: Carefully weigh the pros and cons about disclosing your status. Talk with your doctor or a therapist, or call an AIDS hot line to discuss all potential ramifications.

Rule: Find a local support group for recently diagnosed individuals with HIV. Think about attending.

Rule: If you choose to tell certain people, be prepared for a wide range of responses—from support to abandonment. Before any discussion, gather some

AIDS/HIV *pamphlets to give to less knowledgeable family members or friends; that way you needn't be the expert at the very moment you need support.*

Rule: *Be aware that the more people you tell, the more difficult it becomes to control that information. Make decisions on a case-by-case basis. Do what works for you.*

"I have often seen men prove unmannerly by too much manners and importunate by too much courtesy."

—MONTAIGNE

What to Say When a Friend Tests Positive

If a friend tells you that he is HIV-positive, he is evidencing great confidence and trust in you. When your friend is telling you the news, listen carefully and pick up on as many cues as he gives you. Is he despondent, terrified, in denial, or okay? Try to hear what he is saying and respond to his needs.

By telling you, your friend is breaking through his denial. Don't let your own denial color what you say. Don't be a Pollyanna. Don't say, "Everything will be all right." The most appropriate response is probably "Oh, shit!" Tell him you are there for him and will be there. And *be there!* Tell him you will help him get all the information he needs. Tell him that for every individual with HIV the disease takes its own course at its own pace.

Rule: *Show concern and compassion. Ask whether you can do anything for him. Mean it. Don't make promises you can't keep. Be realistic about the extent of your involvement in your friend's illness. If you know others who have tested positive or any long-term survivors, talk about their examples and offer to introduce them (ask those other friends first, of course).*

Rule: *Make yourself available to help your friend, but let him call the shots. Volunteer to do research. What treatments, if any, are recommended at his stage of disease? Are there any experimental treatments that he should know about? Government benefits programs? Questions about health insurance? Would he like you to put together a list of support groups?*

Rule: *With all the changes that such a diagnosis is apt to bring, try to keep as many things the same as before. As a person becomes more ill, be vigilant in including him in activities you've shared before. From time to time, tell him you're thinking about his health and that you remain open to listen, talk, or gather information.*

Rule: *Don't run away. Don't avoid him. If you are worried—about your own health or his health—talk about your feelings with someone else who can help you sort through them. If your friend is in crisis himself, don't burden him with your concerns at the same time.*

"*Among mortals second thoughts are wisest.*"

—EURIPIDES

HIV and the Law

The cornerstone of federal protection for people with HIV disease is the Americans with Disabilities Act (ADA), an important piece of civil rights legislation that protects people with many disabilities from discrimination—at work, in schools, in hospitals, in most places where business is conducted or services are provided.

The ADA provides specific protections to people with HIV disease. An employer cannot refuse to hire a person who is HIV-infected. Nor can such a person be fired for this reason. This act also requires employers to make "reasonable accommodations" to people with HIV disease regarding their workplace responsibilities.

Rule: An employer cannot treat a person with HIV disease or AIDS any differently because of the illness.

Rule: In almost any professional situation (and locale), it is illegal for an employer to ask an employee's HIV status.

> *"It is almost a definition of a gentleman to say that he is one who never inflicts pain."*
>
> —John Henry Cardinal Newman

Asking about HIV Status

Dennis and Kyle are kissing passionately in the hallway as Dennis fumbles with his keys, finally unlatching the door. Kyle uses his foot to shove the door closed as they begin tugging at each other's clothes. "You're so handsome," Dennis murmurs, unbuttoning Kyle's shirt. They move toward the bedroom, but make it only as far as the living-room floor. After more kissing, Dennis says, "I'm negative by the way." Kyle pauses and averts his eyes.

Some men think that another's HIV status is absolutely not their business, and such information has no impact on their sexual behavior. Others say that before sex they want to know a man's HIV status or to reveal their own. Says Roy, an HIV-negative man: "I've lost two lovers to AIDS in five years and I have to say I'm just not prepared to meet another man who may become sick and die in the near future. Before asking a guy out, I try to figure out whether he's positive or has been ill, but, if I can't, I will ask." Samuel, who has AIDS, says, "I always tell a potential sex partner of my HIV status. I want the information out there. I don't want to get involved with a man who can't handle my situation. I've been burned enough times during the epidemic by HIV-negative men who only want to date 'their own kind.' Also, I think potential sex partners have a right to know."

Still, many men in the gay community are adamant that a person's HIV status is a private matter—even when it comes to sex partners. Says John: "Because I have safe sex all the time, I don't feel any obligation to disclose my status. In the same light, I don't feel there's any reason for a potential date or sex partner to ask me the question. It's none of his business. It won't make any difference to what happens."

Rule: If you feel you need to ask, ask—but ask yourself some questions first. How will this information affect you? Will it affect how you proceed with the relationship? Will it affect your sexual practices? Remember, people disclose what they want others to know when they want them to know it. In asking, be prepared for any possible response—including anger and rejection. Be prepared not to get the information you were seeking. Think about what you will do then.

Rule: Because you want to discuss HIV status, don't assume he does. He may not be ready to disclose the information or simply may not know. Don't ask this question half-naked or in the throes of passion.

Rule: At some point, every HIV-infected individual must disclose this information to a partner he cares about—sometime between the first kiss and the first anniversary. This revelation (if it is one) is not about safe sex, but intimacy and honesty. Whether HIV-negative or -positive, the foundation of a healthy and honest relationship is openness and trust.

Rule: *If you have information about a person's HIV status and it is generally not known to others, don't disclose it to anyone else.*

DOCTOR AND HOSPITAL ETIQUETTE

The Importance of Asking Questions

There are those who enter a doctor's office thinking it somehow rude or pushy to take out a list of prepared questions. While this kind of "interview" would be considered a *faux pas* in social situations, that is absolutely untrue in a doctor-patient context, and any good doctor will encourage you to ask all your questions (as long as he or she has time).

In choosing a new doctor, Gay Men's Health Crisis tells prospective patients to consider these questions:

- Is the doctor willing to take an aggressive approach with your illness? Will he encourage you to become as informed as you can and want to be about new drugs and treatments? Will he allow you to take an active role in all decision making?

- Is the doctor experienced in getting patients into new drug trials (if appropriate) or new research protocols? Will he monitor you in such protocols?

- Is he (and are you) interested in exploring alternatives to established Western medicine, for instance, homeopathy, vitamin therapies, treatments not approved by the Food and Drug Administration, and macrobiotic diets?

- Will the doctor follow your wishes with regard to ending life support or establishing a living will?

Rule: If you are not pleased with your doctor, ask friends or a local AIDS agency for other referrals. Never stay with a doctor because you think it would be "rude" or wrong to leave him or her. It is extremely important that you trust your doctor, have confidence in his or her medical skills and knowledge, and feel that he or she respects your sexual orientation (and that he or she respects your relationship if you're in one).

Bringing a Friend Along to the Doctor

There's also a good deal of uncertainty in bringing a friend into the doctor's office—as though he were an uninvited guest. Not true. You may find that bringing a friend along provides you with needed emotional support; he can assist in asking questions and, *very* important, help you remember pertinent information.

Rule: If you bring a friend into the examination room, tell your doctor that he is there to help you. Tell the doctor that anything he or she has to say to you can be said in front of your friend.

When a Friend Is Hospitalized with AIDS

Caleb and Marc had worked together for several years in a publishing house, when Marc was suddenly diagnosed with PCP and hospitalized. Caleb recalls, "I had always been terrified of doctors and hospitals, and now my friend Marc was there and I had to find a way to go visit. I was terrified to go; I didn't know what I would say. Actually, I was really afraid I'd say the wrong thing. Finally I got up my courage and drove over to the medical center. By the time I got in the elevator, my hands were shaking and I thought I'd throw up. I kept asking myself, 'Do I really have to go see him?'"

Rule: When a close friend is ill or hospitalized for an AIDS-related illness, show your concern and affection and find the time to visit (if he is well enough to have visitors). It need not be a long visit; you need not say very much. Your presence is the gift. If he is not a close friend, send a card or call.

Rule: If he is seriously ill, do not telephone his room. If you desire up-to-date information or want to relay a message, call the nurses' station or a mutual friend. Ask to be told when it will be appropriate to call.

Rule: *Send or drop off a gift, either a bouquet of fresh flowers, a blooming plant (check with the nurses' station first about bringing in flowers or plants; some people with AIDS cannot tolerate them), chocolates, your friend's favorite magazines, or a CD or tape.*

Rule: *When in a hospital room, keep your voice low. Don't overstay your welcome. Be considerate of your friend and any others present.*

Rule: *As much as everyone wants a happy outcome, it does no good to tell blatant untruths to your friend. If your friend looks awful, don't say, "You look great." Similarly, if the disease is fairly progressed, it's pointless to say, "You'll be fine in no time!" On the other hand, don't become the voice of doom and gloom.*

Rule: *Stay involved. Be consistent. Ask if you can help out at home: clean the apartment, pick up the mail, take care of the dog, pay the bills. There are many ways that you can be useful to your friend.*

Rule: *If you're visiting a friend who has been in the hospital for a long time, consider dropping off a small gift for the nurses. These men and women are on the front lines and deserve thanks and appreciation. Conversely, if your friend is being mistreated or neglected, don't hesitate to complain on his behalf.*

A Lengthy Illness

AIDS is not like having a heart attack, in which there's a crisis, you deal with it, it's over. HIV-infection is a long-term illness requiring either the periodic or constant attention of friends, coworkers and loved ones. Says Luis: "I had worked for my boss for three years when he was diagnosed with PCP. Unfortunately, he had a very bad case, and it took him several weeks to rally. Almost immediately, he came down with another opportunistic infection, again requiring a lengthy hospital stay. I realized that it would make sense to organize his friends and coworkers into a support team, with two people designated to take care of him each night of the week. After getting the green light from him, I invited everyone over to my apartment to talk about how they could help. I was so amazed by their commitment. This method really worked out over the long run."

Rule: *Continue to plan activities with your friend (if he is able). In planning an activity, be sensitive to your friend's energy level and well-being. Let him make the decisions about what you'll be doing.*

Rule: *After each visit, plan the next one. This will provide a sense of continuity and security for your friend. Always call before going to visit—even if it is a regularly scheduled visit—if only to find out if your friend needs something picked up on the way over. If, for some reason, you must change your plans, let your friend know as soon as possible and make plans for another visit right away.*

Rule: Be a good listener. Let him set the agenda. Don't try
to change the topic. Ask questions that you think
will help clarify his thinking. If his problems or
emotions become too entangled, recommend that he
get additional support—from an AIDS hot line, a
support group, or private therapy.

Rule: Don't forget to take care of yourself—emotionally
and physically. If you don't, you won't be an effec-
tive friend over the long run.

"We won't die secret deaths anymore."

—Tony Kushner

On Death and Dying

Although every etiquette book addresses—in depth—
the question of funerals and memorial services, none of
them tackles the extremely painful process of how we live
as our friends are dying. Death is not a topic that comes
easily to us; even after so many losses from AIDS, many
people say they find each new death to be shocking.

With AIDS you often witness the gradual (or sometimes rapid) decline of a person you love or care about.
He may lose weight, hair, eyesight, develop painful
rashes, and become afflicted with herpes sores. There
may be mental deterioration as well. He may become
less alert, less articulate, and may lose interest in the
world. He may become angry and depressed. It may
become difficult and painful for you to stay close while

your friend is dying. It is not uncommon to have the urge to run away or to hide.

Rule: Do your absolute best to remain close to your friend. If you've come this far, your friend needs to know he can continue to count on you—that you will hold him, touch him, comfort him, and love him.

Rule: Be prepared for a life-threatening crisis. If it's at your place, alert the appropriate people that a crisis is occurring and that they're invited to visit. (If you receive such a call, act promptly.)

Rule: Continue to talk to him (even if he's unconscious). Tell him you're there. Read to him from scripture or pray aloud with him (if that is part of his beliefs). Comb his hair. Stroke his skin. Hold him.

FUNERALS AND MEMORIAL SERVICES

Notifying Friends and Family of a Death

Upon death, there are a great many details to be taken care of immediately. If the deceased is known to have made his wishes clear regarding funeral services and any other matters, those instructions should be retrieved as soon as possible so they can be followed. (Everyone, but especially one with a life-threatening disease, should take the time to make directives regarding legal and financial matters, write a living will, and leave funeral instructions.)

As soon as is possible, someone close to the deceased should be designated or should assume responsibility to coordinate the various tasks and events. (This may be a close friend, a business partner, a sibling, or a parent. If possible, it should not be the deceased's lover or the closest survivor because, presumably, his grief is the most overwhelming. No matter who, honor the directives of the deceased.) The point person should start by making a list of the various tasks to be accomplished and then designating volunteers to fulfill them. The responsibility falls to him to ensure that the deceased's wishes are being followed and that all tasks are completed in a timely way.

Rule: Notify all family members, appropriate friends, and colleagues of the deceased by telephone of the death and the funeral or memorial service arrangements. Divide the list among a few good friends. While this is never an easy phone call to make, it becomes easier as you call friend after friend. You might say, "Grace, this is Hal. I have some sad news. Marco died last night at home surrounded by his lover and his immediate family. Funeral services will be held the day after tomorrow at Lyman Brothers Funeral Home at 10 A.M. We hope to see you."

Rule: Don't leave death messages on voice mail or answering machines. Either leave no message and call back or leave a message identifying yourself as a friend of the deceased, asking the recipient to call back as soon as possible.

Rule: Notify the deceased's employer and place of employment and, if appropriate, the grieving survivor's employer as well.

Rule: Designate someone to provide correct information regarding funeral arrangements and to log all incoming messages (these include telegrams and mailgrams, letters, hand-delivered condolence notes, faxes, mass cards), as well as flower arrangements and gifts of food. If a private funeral is planned, callers should be notified and thanked for expressing their concern. Send thank-you notes to everyone for his or her sympathy.

Finding a Funeral Home

In most cities throughout the country with large gay communities, there are a number of funeral homes known to be gay-friendly (if not gay-owned) and experienced in dealing with deaths from AIDS. If you find yourself in a situation where you do not know the name of a funeral home, call your local AIDS service organization and ask for referrals. You also can turn to one of the gay newspapers in your community and go through the obituaries section to see which funeral homes are most frequently used. In other places, the person arranging the funeral should make some preliminary calls—either to the deceased's doctor, pastor, or the local hospital for the names of recommended homes.

It is also important to choose a funeral home where all budgets can be accommodated. Avoid an elaborate funeral or memorial that leaves a lover or family members in debt. For some time now, the trend has been toward simple funerals—even among people who could afford more elaborate ones.

The Death Certificate

Although this matter is usually handled by the funeral director, be sure that multiple copies of the death certificate are obtained. The certificate will be needed for collecting insurance, closing bank accounts, and probating the estate. Each copy must be stamped and signed by the coroner's office.

Death Notices

There are several kinds of death notices to be considered. One kind is a paid obituary placed in the local newspaper. As soon as is possible, such a death notice should be phoned in to the city desk. Following is a sample death notice:

> **COOPER, Kenneth Lane.** On Sept. 30, 1994, age 34, after a long battle with AIDS. Beloved companion and life partner of Jason Mandell, devoted son of Margery and Marshall Cooper. Brother of Randolph, Peter, and Jeremy Cooper. Friends may call at Frank E. Campbell, 1076 Madison Ave. at 81st St., Saturday, 1–4 P.M. Service at the Ethical Culture Society, 2 West 64th St., Monday at 11 A.M. Interment at Chapel of the Chimes Cemetery, Lafayette, CA, Friday at 2 P.M. Contributions may be made, in lieu of flowers, to the AIDS Project Contra Costa, 2280 Diamond Blvd., Concord, CA 94520.

Rule: It is not required that you state the deceased's age in a death notice. It is a matter of personal preference. Whether or not you state the cause of death is also a personal matter.

Rule: Honor the deceased's primary relationship (when relevant and possible). In most large city newspapers, expect to encounter difficulty in using gay-specific language to describe the deceased and his closest survivor (particularly the word "lover"). At the time of this writing, even The New York Times *doesn't consider that word fit to print.*

Rule: If the survivors do not wish other people to go to the cemetery for the burial, omit the interment notice from the announcement. If the survivors also want the funeral to be closed to the public, the announcement should say "Funeral private."

Rule: If it was the intention of the deceased that contributions be made to a specific charity, the organization should be listed (with its address) at the end of the paid notice.

Obituaries are written for prominent individuals by newspaper staffs. (In small towns, everyone typically gets a free obituary.) Often, if the individual is very prominent, an obituary may have been prepared to run at the time of death (for instance, many newspapers had prepared obituaries for Rock Hudson and Randy Shilts). If

an obituary has not been prepared, the following information should be provided to the appropriate reporter
(all facts should be checked with a partner or family
member).

Name and address of the deceased

Date and place of death

Cause of death

Name of partner (if relevant) and/or other survivors
and their relationship to the deceased

Place of birth

Place of employment and job title

Education

Military service

Community service

Corporate directorships

Major awards

Titles of published works, including books, plays,
films, songs

Details of funeral or memorial service and interment

Contact person and telephone number

Another type of notice is a recent adaptation of the
paid announcement and the newspaper obituary. Many
gay newspapers now take obituaries that are prepared by
the deceased's loved ones. These notices, generally free,

focus more on community involvements and are less formal than either of the other notices. Contact your local gay newspaper for more information.

Flowers or Donations?

The death notice often makes the wishes of the survivors clear on this question. "In lieu of flowers, donations may be made to . . ." In the community, it's become customary for AIDS and gay-related nonprofits to be the beneficiaries of these gifts, although any charitable cause may be designated. More than one charity also may be listed.

> "There is no grief like the grief
> which does not speak."
>
> —HENRY W. LONGFELLOW

What to Say?

Very few people know what to say to the bereaved during the mourning period. If you telephone, attend a wake, or visit the immediate survivors, you need say only a few words and stay a short time. Generally, it is appropriate to explain how sorry you are to hear this sad news, how much you liked or loved the deceased, how he will be missed, and what a personal loss you feel. If the illness has been particularly long and arduous (as it generally is with AIDS), acknowledge how

much the deceased suffered and that the suffering is
now over.

Rule: *Don't be afraid to show your emotions, especially
grief. While grief is often very painful, the more you
try to avoid it, the longer your mourning can take.*

Rule: *Offer assistance to the bereaved in specific terms.
May I come over and make dinner for you on
Wednesday? May I take care of the apartment while
you are away? Let me call you later in the week to
see what I can do for you. Stay involved.*

Rule: *If you feel the bereaved would benefit from a
bereavement group (found in many cities), offer to
get information for him.*

> ## "More tears have been shed
> over men's lack of manners
> than their lack of morals."
>
> —HELEN HATHAWAY

Family Trouble

"From the moment Guillermo was diagnosed, his family refused to have contact with him," recalls his lover,
Marty. "We were both incredibly angry and hurt, but
after eighteen months of this kind of treatment, we got

used to it. When Guillermo became very ill toward the end, I called his brother to let the family know that he would probably die over the weekend. They were polite, although I didn't hear back from them. When Guillermo died, I had a close friend notify his family and—to my great consternation—they actually attended the funeral. Now, they are suing me for Guillermo's estate."

If any potential for conflict exists between a surviving lover and the deceased's family, an attorney should be consulted early on to safeguard your friend's wishes. Depending on the state, your will should state explicitly who is designated to carry out your last wishes, including funeral arrangements. Also, in some states it makes sense to designate a lover or a close friend as your legal and/or medical power of attorney to further prevent others from stepping in after your death.

Rule: Take the lead in facing potential family problems. Know your rights. Talk to an attorney.

Rule: Always honor the deceased as best you can.

"This is my last message to you; in sorrow seek happiness."

—FYODOR DOSTOEVSKY

Planning a Funeral

Ronny had always known what kind of funeral he wanted. He did not want some gloomy, sad event; if anything, he wanted it to be gay and festive. When mourners entered the church for his service, they saw a phalanx of bright-colored balloons sitting as a backdrop to the lectern. A good friend of Ronny's—a professional soloist—sang "Somewhere over the Rainbow" as the opening song. After a brief welcome, Ronny's best friend, Carolyn, herself ill with AIDS, walked slowly to the lectern to deliver the eulogy Ronny had asked her to prepare. For a time she stood staring at the mourners, her eyes glistening, her body leaning heavily on the lectern. Then, in simple, loving words, Carolyn told Ronny's friends and family how much she loved him and how much she would miss him. She then asked anyone else who cared to remember Ronny publicly to come forward and do so. Nearly a dozen men and women queued up to give their remembrances; some cried, some joked, some read poetry. . . . Said Carolyn later: "All of Ronny's friends provided insight into a different part of his personality and life, so that by the end it was really like he was complete and whole. It was wonderful."

As the service ended, the balloons were untied and taken outside. Carolyn asked everyone to beam a message up to Ronny as they released the balloons into the brilliant afternoon sky. Slowly, the colorful arrangement drifted higher and higher until it disappeared forever from view.

Funerals are for the survivors, but should be designed to reflect and honor the life of the deceased. If it is an entirely unexpected death, grief may well be the predominant theme. However, many who die from AIDS have the opportunity to discuss the kind of funeral they would like (or not like): celebratory, political, private, very public. The music and the eulogy or eulogies should reflect the overall theme chosen by the deceased or the most bereaved.

Rule: *Ushers are usually close friends, colleagues, or family members of the deceased, and they help seat attendees. It is an honor to be asked to be an usher. Ushers should direct people toward the front of the church or hall, reserving the first several rows for the closest friends and family members.*

Rule: *If the deceased was prominent in his community, four to ten honorary pallbearers may be chosen (these days both men and women serve as honorary pallbearers) to precede the casket in and out of the church, walking in twos. If the casket is already present in the church, the pallbearers enter just before the start of the service. Honorary pallbearers are generally distinguished members of the community as well as close friends of the deceased.*

Rule: *Those chosen to give eulogies—or some formal remarks—should bear in mind the deceased's wishes for the tone and tenor of the service. If it is a religious service, a minister or rabbi will probably speak, but any number of individuals may deliver remarks. Five to seven minutes is considered the optimal length for remarks of this nature. If, while speaking, you begin to cry, allow yourself some time to recover. If you cannot, it's best to simply say, "I'm sorry," and leave the lectern. People will understand.*

Memorial Services

Memorial services are generally held within a month of a person's death, always after the deceased has been interred or cremated. A memorial service affords friends and family members from far afield the opportunity to attend. Since many people with AIDS are cremated shortly after death, memorial services have become increasingly common in the gay community. As with a funeral, a clergyman or friend or colleague may preside, with any number of people speaking. Following the service, it is customary for friends and family to take light refreshments in an adjoining room or to reconvene at the deceased's or a friend's house for a light meal and conversation about the deceased.

RESOURCES

Ayers, Tess, and Paul Brown. *The Essential Guide to Lesbian and Gay Weddings.* San Francisco: HarperSanFrancisco, 1994.

Baldrige, Letitia. *Letitia Baldrige's Complete Guide to the New Manners for the '90s.* New York: Rawson Associates, 1990.

Boyles, Denis. *The Modern Man's Guide to Modern Women.* New York: HarperCollins, 1993.

Claiborne, Craig. *Elements of Etiquette: A Guide to Table Manners in an Imperfect World.* New York: William Morrow, 1992.

Feinberg, Steven L., ed. *Crane's Blue Book of Stationery, Tiffany Edition.* New York: Doubleday, 1989.

Hix, Charles. *Dressing Right*. New York: St. Martin's Press, 1978.

Martin, April. *The Lesbian and Gay Parenting Handbook*. New York: HarperCollins, 1993.

Martin, Judith. *Miss Manners' Guide for the Turn-of-the-Millennium*. New York: Pharos Books, 1989.

———. *Miss Manners' Guide to Excruciatingly Correct Behavior*. New York: Warner Books, 1983.

Petrow, Steven, et al. *When Someone You Know Has AIDS: A Practical Guide* (revised and updated edition). New York: Crown Publishers, 1993.

Preston, John. *The Big Gay Book: A Man's Survival Guide for the 90's*. New York: Plume, 1991.

Richardson, Donald Charles. *Men of Style: The Zoli Guide for the Total Man*. New York: Villard Books, 1992.

Zunin, Leonard M., and Hilary Stanton Zunin. *The Art of Condolence*. New York: HarperCollins, 1991.

ACKNOWLEDGMENTS

I'm grateful to the following people who helped me to write this book:

David Rakoff, my editor, whose constant belief in me steadied my hand and focused my thoughts, and whose friendship and good nature are without equal;

Charlotte Sheedy, my agent, who has taught me so much about "doing the right thing";

Ronald Mark Kraft, editor-in-chief of *Genre* magazine, who made my manners column a reality and edits me the old-fashioned way—with a sharp pencil, an expansive mind, and good humor;

David Shiver, who is always there for me;

Scott Hafner, friend and gentleman defined in one;

Paul Di Donato and Daniel Cawley, who challenge me,

make me laugh, and keep me from going completely insane;

Craig Lyall and Dom DiMento, who hosted the dinner where the idea for this book was born;

Nick Steele, my cowriter, whose enthusiasm and dedication carried us through;

Bruce Cronander, who fine-tunes my manners and my manners column;

Cynthia Perry, whose humor never flags, whose wisdom is legendary, and whose friendship is priceless;

Barry Owen, who held me by night and sang to me by day;

Julie Petrow and Jay Petrow, my sister and brother, and my parents, Richard and Margot, for their support and love.

I'd also like to thank the following individuals for their specific contributions: William D. Glenn, MFCC (Continuum HIV Day Services), Joe Fera (San Francisco AIDS Foundation), Peter Minichiello, Tricia Foster, Susan Ostwald Barnes, Charlotte Eyerman, Lori Grinker, Barry Raine, Mark Illeman, Chris Duncan, Fred Silverman, Greg Riley, Nancy Clarke, Maddy Cohen, Eric Wilson, James D. Woods and Paul Young, David Tuller, Betsy Nolan, Peter Poulos, Peter Stein, the staff and owners of San Francisco's Universal Cafe, The Gauntlet, and Tiffany & Co.

STEVEN PETROW
SAN FRANCISCO
APRIL 1995

To Steven Petrow, a learned man, patient teacher, and true gentleman. For your vision and grace under fire, I sincerely thank you.

I'd also like to acknowledge the following people for their time and expertise: Bob and Rod Jackson-Paris, Greg D. Mathos (Hugo Boss Collections), Eric Graham (Macy's), Erica Gavin (Barneys New York), Bob Thomas (Nordstrom), Scott Thomas (Harlow Salon), Will Lippincott (*The New Yorker*), Tracy Schwab (Uptown Caterers), Gary Floyd (The Leather Rack, Washington, D.C.), Mitch Kessler and Adam Selene (Adam and Jillian Sensual Whips and Toys, Copiague, New York), Bob Harden (Mr. Leather, San Francisco), and to the following Washington escorts: James, Chuck, Jerry, Christian, and Danny.

NICK STEELE
NEW YORK CITY
APRIL 1995

ACKNOWLEDGMENTS

217

INDEX

semiresident, at summer
shares, 142
with special diets, 129–30

Hair care, 176–77
Hair loss, 176–77
Halloween, 34–35
Hamper, 84
Hand-holding, 19, 20
Hate crimes, 32
Hathaway, Helen, 207
Heterosexuals, 3
HIV status, 185–94. *See also*
AIDS
asking about, 192–94
deciding to take an HIV anti-
body test, 186–87
disclosure of, 188, 189
if you (or a friend) test posi-
tive, 187–91
the law and, 191
Hoffer, Eric, 75
Holding hands, 19, 20
Holidays, 34–36
Home crises, dealing with, at
work, 29–30
Homophobia, 91
in the workplace, 30–32
Horace, 25
Hosts. *See also* Entertaining;
Parties
introductions by, 5
Houseguests, 134–36
at summer shares, 142–43
Housewarming, 83
"How are you?"
answering the question,
10–11
asking someone who is ill, 11
"How do I look?," answering the
question, 179–81
Hugo, Victor, 20

Humphrey, Hubert H., 33
Hustlers, bar, 72
Hygiene, 175

Illness. *See also* AIDS; HIV status
of a loved one, 29–30
Interment notice, 204
Interrupting to introduce yourself, 9
Introductions (introducing),
4–13
avoiding, 8
guests to one another, 5
by hosts, 5
"inferiors" to "superiors," 5
remembering names, 5
term to use for your guy in,
11–13
uncomfortable, 8
when not required, 9
when unable to remember
names, 6–8
your new boyfriend to your ex,
5–6
yourself, 5
interruptions and, 9
when someone is leaving,
8–9
Invitations
to ceremonies of commitment,
91–97
addressing the invitation,
96
less formal, 94
more formal, 92–93
names on, 94–95
responding to, 99
when to choose, and mail
invitations, order, 97
to charity events, 20–21
to gay couples, 143–44

ABOUT THE AUTHORS

Steven Petrow is the author of three books, including *Dancing Against the Darkness: A Journey Through America in the Age of AIDS* and *When Someone You Know Has AIDS: A Practical Guide*. The recipient of numerous writing grants, including awards from the National Endowment for the Humanities and the Smithsonian Institution, he has written for several national magazines, among them *Life, Longevity,* and *The Advocate*. He is editor in chief of *10 Percent* magazine and lives in San Francisco.

Nick Steele is an editor with *Art & Understanding Magazine,* an active freelance journalist, and currently writing his first novel. He has been a gay rights advocate, dedicated volunteer, and AIDS activist for many years. He lives in New York City.